# 15 Days of Prayer
# With Thomas Merton

Also in this collection:

André Dupleix,
*15 Days of Prayer*
*With Teilhard de Chardin*

Michel Lafon,
*15 Days of Prayer*
*With Charles de Foucauld*

Constant Tonnelier,
*15 Days of Prayer*
*With Saint Thérèse of Lisieux*

François Vayne,
*15 Days of Prayer*
*With Saint Bernadette of Lourdes*

# 15 DAYS OF PRAYER

## WITH

# Thomas Merton

ANDRÉ GOZIER, O.S.B.

Translated by Victoria Hébert and Denis Sabourin

Liguori

LIGUORI, MISSOURI

Published by Liguori Publications
Liguori, Missouri
http://www.liguori.org

This book is a translation of *Prier 15 Jours Avec Thomas Merton*, or *L'unité conquise*, published by Nouvelle Cité, 1996, Montrouge, France.

**Library of Congress Cataloging-in-Publication Data**

Gozier, André.
    [Prier 15 jours avec Thomas Merton. English]
    15 days of prayer with Thomas Merton / André Gozier ; translated by Victoria Hébert and Denis Sabourin. — 1st English ed.
    p.  cm.
    Includes bibliographical references.
    ISBN 0-7648-0491-X (pbk.)
    1. Merton, Thomas, 1915–1968 Meditations. 2. Spiritual life—Catholic Church Meditations. I. Title. II. Title: Fifteen days of prayer with Thomas Merton.
BX4705.M542G6913  1999
269'.6—dc21                          99–22526

Printed in the United States of America
03 02 01 00 99   5 4 3 2 1
First English Edition 1999

# Table of Contents

# How to Use This Book

AN OLD CHINESE PROVERB, or at least what I am able to recall of what is supposed to be an old Chinese proverb, goes something like this: "Even a journey of a thousand miles begins with a single step." When you think about it, the truth of the proverb is obvious. It is impossible to begin any project, let alone a journey, without taking the first step. I think it might also be true, although I cannot recall if another Chinese proverb says it, "that the first step is often the hardest." Or, as someone else once observed, "the distance between a thought and the corresponding action needed to implement the idea takes the most energy." I don't know who shared that perception with me but I am certain it was not an old Chinese master!

With this ancient proverbial wisdom, and the not-so-ancient wisdom of an unknown contemporary sage still fresh, we move from proverbs to presumptions. How do these relate to the task before us?

I am presuming that if you are reading this introduction it is because you are contemplating a journey. My presumption is that you are preparing for a spiritual journey and that you have taken at least some of the first steps necessary to prepare for this journey. I also presume, and please excuse me if I am making too many presumptions, that in your preparation for the spiritual journey you have determined that you need a guide. From deep within the recesses of your deepest self, there was something that called you to consider Thomas Merton as a potential companion. If my presumptions are correct, may I congratulate you on this decision? I think you have made a wise choice, a choice that can be confirmed by yet another source of wisdom, the wisdom that comes from practical experience.

Even an informal poll of experienced travelers will reveal a common opinion; it is very difficult to travel alone. Some might observe that it is even foolish. Still others may be even stronger in their opinion and go so far as to insist that it is necessary to have a guide, especially when you are traveling into uncharted waters and into territory that you have not yet experienced. I am of the personal opinion that a traveling companion is welcome under all circumstances. The thought of traveling alone, to some exciting destination without someone to share the journey with does not capture my imagination or channel my enthusiasm. However, with that being noted, what is simply a matter of preference on the normal journey becomes a matter of necessity when a person embarks on a spiritual journey.

The spiritual journey, which can be the most challenging of all journeys, is experienced best with a guide, a companion, or at the very least, a friend in whom you have placed your trust. This observation is not a preference or an opinion but rather an established spiritual necessity. All of the great saints with whom I am familiar had a spiritual director or a confessor that journeyed with them. Admittedly, at times the saint might well have traveled far beyond the experience of their guide and companion but more often than not they would return to their director and reflect on their experience. Understood in this sense, the director and companion provided a valuable contribution and necessary resource.

When I was learning how to pray (a necessity for anyone who desires to be a full-time and public "religious person"), the community of men that I belong to gave me a great gift. Between my second and third year in college, I was given a one-year sabbatical, with all expenses paid and all of my personal needs met. This period of time was called novitiate. I was officially designated as a novice, a beginner in the spiritual journey, and I was assigned a "master," a person who was willing to lead me. In addition to the master, I was provided with every imaginable book and any other resource that I could possibly need. Even with all that I was provided, I did not learn how to pray because of the books and the unlimited resources, rather it was the master, the companion who was the key to the experience.

One day, after about three months of reading, of quiet and solitude, and of practicing all of the methods and descriptions of prayer that were available to me, the master called. "Put away the books, forget the method, and just listen." We went into a room, became quiet, and tried to recall the presence of God, and then, the master simply prayed out loud and permitted me to listen to his prayer. As he prayed, he revealed his hopes, his dreams, his struggles, his successes, and most of all, his relationship with God. I discovered as I listened that his prayer was deeply intimate but most of all it was self-revealing. As I learned about him, I was led through his life experience to the place where God dwells. At that moment I was able to understand a little bit about what I was supposed to do if I really wanted to pray.

The dynamic of what happened when the master called, invited me to listen, and then revealed his innermost self to me as he communicated with God in prayer, was important. It wasn't so much that the master was trying to reveal to me what needed to be said; he was not inviting me to pray with the same words that he used, but rather that he was trying to bring me to that place within myself where prayer becomes possible. That place, a place of intimacy and of self-awareness, was a necessary stop on the journey and it was a place that I needed to be led to. I could not have easily discovered it on my own.

The purpose of the volume that you hold in your hand is to lead you, over a period of fifteen days or, maybe more realistically, fifteen prayer periods, to a place where prayer is possible. If you already have a regular experience and practice of prayer, perhaps this volume can help lead you to a deeper place, a more intimate relationship with the Lord.

It is important to note that the purpose of this book is not to lead you to a better relationship with Thomas Merton, your spiritual companion. Although your companion will invite you to share some of their deepest and most intimate thoughts, your companion is doing so only to bring you to that place where God dwells. After all, the true measurement of a companion for the journey is that they bring you to the place where you need to be, and then they step back, out of the picture. A guide who brings you to the desired destination and then sticks around is a very unwelcome guest!

Many times I have found myself attracted to a particular idea or method for accomplishing a task, only to discover that what seemed to be inviting and helpful possessed too many details. All of my energy went to the mastery of the details and I soon lost my enthusiasm. In each instance, the book that seemed so promising ended up on my book-shelf, gathering dust. I can assure you, it is not our intention that this book end up on your bookcase, filled with promise, but unable to deliver.

There are three simple rules that need to be followed in order to use this book with a measure of satisfaction.

*Place:* It is important that you choose a place for reading that provides the necessary atmosphere for reflection and that does not provide too many distractions. Whatever place you choose needs to be comfortable, have the necessary lighting, and, finally, have a sense of "welcoming" about it. You need to be able to look forward to the experience of the journey. Don't travel steerage if you know you will be more comfortable in first class and if the choice is realistic for you. On the other hand, if first class is a distraction and you feel more comfortable and more yourself in steerage, then it is in steerage that you belong.

My favorite place is an overstuffed and comfortable chair in my bedroom. There is a light over my shoulder, and the chair reclines if I feel a need to recline. Once in a while, I get lucky and the sun comes through my window and bathes the entire room in light. I have other options and other places that are available to me but this is the place that I prefer.

*Time:* Choose a time during the day when you are most alert and when you are most receptive to reflection, meditation, and prayer. The time that you choose is an essential component. If you are a morning person, for example, you should choose a time that is in the morning. If you are more alert in the afternoon, choose an afternoon time slot; and if evening is your preference, then by all means choose the evening. Try to avoid "peak" periods in your daily routine when you know that you might be disturbed. The time that you choose needs to be your time and needs to work for you.

It is also important that you choose how much time you will spend with your companion each day. For some it will be possible to set aside enough time in order to read and reflect on all the material that is offered for a given day. For others, it might not be possible to devote one time to the suggested material for the day, so the prayer period may need to be extended for two, three, or even more sessions. It is not important how long it takes you; it is only important that it works for you and that you remain committed to that which is possible.

For myself I have found that fifteen minutes in the early morning, while I am still in my robe and pajamas and before my morning coffee, and even before I prepare myself for the day, is the best time. No one expects to see me or to interact with me because I have not yet "announced" the fact that I am awake or even on the move. However, once someone hears me in the bathroom, then my window of opportunity is gone. It is therefore important to me that I use the time that I have identified when it is available to me.

*Freedom:* It may seem strange to suggest that freedom is the third necessary ingredient, but I have discovered that it is most important. By freedom I understand a certain "stance toward life," a "permission to be myself and to be gentle and understanding of who I am." I am constantly amazed at how the human person so easily sets himself or herself up for disappointment and perceived failure. We so easily make judgments about ourselves and our actions and our choices, and very often those judgments are negative, and not at all helpful.

For instance, what does it really matter if I have chosen a place and a time, and I have missed both the place and the time for three days in a row? What does it matter if I have chosen, in that twilight time before I am completely awake and still a little sleepy, to roll over and to sleep for fifteen minutes more? Does it mean that I am not serious about the journey, that I really don't want to pray, that I am just fooling myself when I say that my prayer time is important to me? Perhaps, but I prefer to believe that it simply means that I am tired and I just wanted a little more sleep. It doesn't mean anything more than that. However, if I make it mean more than that, then I can become discouraged, frustrated, and put myself into a state where I might more easily give up. "What's the use? I might as well forget all about it."

The same sense of freedom applies to the reading and the praying of this text. If I do not find the introduction to each day helpful, I don't need to read it. If I find the questions for reflection at the end of the reflection repetitive, then I should choose to close the book and go my own way. Even if I discover that the reflection offered for the day is not the one that I prefer and that the one for the next day seems more inviting, then by all means, go on to the one for the next day.

That's it! If you apply these simple rules to your journey you should receive the maximum benefit and you will soon find yourself at your destination. But be prepared to be surprised. If you have never been on a spiritual journey you should know that the "travel brochures" and the other descriptions that you might have heard are nothing compared to the real thing. There is so much more than you can imagine.

A final prayer of blessing suggests itself:

> Lord, catch me off guard today.
> Surprise me with some moment of beauty
>     or pain
> So that at least for the moment
> I may be startled into seeing that you are here
>     in all your splendor,
> Always and everywhere,
> Barely hidden,
> Beneath,
> Beyond,
> Within this life I breathe.
>
> —*Frederick Buechner*

REV. THOMAS M. SANTA, CSSR
LIGUORI, MISSOURI
FEAST OF THE PRESENTATION, 1999

# A Brief Chronology
# of Thomas Merton's Life

1915   Born to Owen Merton and Ruth Jenkins Merton on January 31 in Prades, France.

1935   Enters Columbia University in New York City.

1939   Receives Master of Arts degree in February; considers studying for the priesthood.

1941   Spends Holy Week in retreat at the Trappist monastery of Our Lady of Gethsemani (in Kentucky). On December 10, enters Gethsemani to become a postulant in the Order of Cistercians of the Strict Observance.

1942   On February 21 receives the habit of a choir-monk novice and is given the religious name of M(ary) Louis.

1944   Takes simple vows on the feast of Saint Joseph (March 19). *Thirty Poems* is published under his secular name. Given writing assignments by the abbot.

1946   Begins to think of a lyrical work but not "pure autobiography" to which he had already given the title *The Seven Storey Mountain* as a tribute to his love for Dante.

1947   Pronounces solemn vows on March 19. Rewrites his autobiography; works on other books.

**1948** *The Seven Storey Mountain* is published; by the following year it is a bestseller.

**1949** Ordained to the priesthood on Ascension Thursday, May 26.

**1951** Appointed master of scholastics. Becomes an American citizen.

**1953** *The Sign of Jonas* published. Interest in moving to a more contemplative life grows as Gethsemani becomes more crowded and occupied with work.

**1955** Becomes master of novices.

**1958** Experiences an "epiphany" at the corner of "Fourth and Walnut" (immortalized in *Conjectures of a Guilty Bystander*) in which he transcends a word-denying mysticism and turns to one that embraces the needs of the world.

**1961** Increasing interest in racial issues and pacifism (publishes prose-poem *Original Child Bomb*); rewrites what will become one of his spiritual classics, *New Seeds of Contemplation*. Intensifies study of Oriental religious thought and Shaker culture.

**1965** On September 8 makes a commitment to the eremitical life

**1968** Leaves abbey on September 10 on first leg of a trip which takes him to the Far East for a meeting on interreligious monastic life in Bangkok. Visits Dalai Lama in northern India and great Buddhist shrines in Sri Lanka. On December 10 gives his paper at a session of the monastic meeting; that afternoon is found dead of an apparent heart attack after having been accidentally electrocuted by a defective fan.

# A Few Notes About Thomas Merton

Man is born with many facets.
His life is successful if he dies unified.

*Paul Valéry*

I don't want to speak to you as an author, or a narrator, not even as a philosopher, but simply as a friend. I would like to speak to you as your alternate self...if you listen, you will hear things that will be said that perhaps are not written in this book. And that will be coming, not from me, but from the One who lives and speaks inside both of us.

*Thomas Merton, from the preface to the*
*Japanese edition of* The Seven Storey Mountain

THOMAS MERTON: A FRIEND, a fellow traveler on life's road. This monk, who experienced a certain renown between 1950 and 1968, is still an important presence in our lives today.

He is present here and now. He is an important presence in France, even if his life experiences were mainly in the United States and Asia. He is an important presence even if years have passed, furtively like the seasons or like the clouds, since the end of his life. Above all, his presence is like a gift. All friends, all good friends, all fellow travelers on life's road are a presence, offered for life, a gift from God. Here and now, he is a real sign of the Absolute Power of God.

All friendships help us cross to the other shore, to enter the Kingdom on the other side of space and time. This book is not about the worship of holy images, relics, or souvenirs, but a means to receive his message. Certain books are true friends, or at least true meeting places, authentic meetings. Authentic, here, as opposed to superficial, that is to say that which does not reach the deeper being.

> I owe a great deal to books, they give me a conversation which never bores me, that never hurts me, they give me the need for silence that they, in turn, nourish, they provide this tranquil happiness which is taken from no one, this indispensable stimulant which they never cease to offer to my mind and, in those times of tragedy, the presence of the Eternal One of whom they are the quest and the sign.
>
> *Maurice Zundel as quoted in*
> Zundel: A Portrait *by Claire Lucques*

In short, *lectio divina* or spiritual reading, which is held dearly in the monastic tradition. That is what Merton's works could bring to us.

What we have here is an encounter with Merton, known by his religious name as Father Louis, or Tom to his friends, who can and should become a friend, a fellow traveler on

the road to the Eternal One. A friend, that is to say, someone who brings us his treasures, another side of ourselves,
someone who we can turn to in our darkest hours, certain
that he will dissipate our blackest clouds. A friend, someone whose presence we enjoy and seek out.

A genuine meeting is rare. It is characterized by the discovery of what we carry hidden inside of ourselves. It is a
revelation of our inner selves. It is unexpected but ob-
scurely awaited. It is illuminating. A true meeting is a
creative power for ourselves. It transforms us. In effect, it
changes our existence, our way of seeing things, our inner
glance. For those who experience a true meeting, there is a
*deeper* self.

All true meetings are registered in sacred stories, in the
sense that they are wanted from God, by God, or at least
permitted by Him. Through these meetings, God enters into
our existence, into our life.

The true meeting unifies our being, contrary to a false
meeting, a nongenuine meeting, which is artificial, superficial, and conventional, in a word, mundane, a meeting which
divides our being.

Communication between two consciousnesses is never
perfect, certainly, but "no man is an island," in the words
of John Donne.

A true meeting is the advancement of consciousness by
creative communication, the ideal condition for spiritual
growth. The true meeting makes us grow. It makes us fulfill
ourselves. A true meeting is a sacrament in the sense that it
is a sign that brings us grace.

As Gilles Farcet said in his book, *Thomas Merton*: "Tom
is linked to my destiny. I attribute many good times, much
passion, and enlightenment to him. He is a part of me and

will never leave me...." An American reader repeats, "Merton speaks as if he is speaking from within me." To write is to create, but it's also to reveal oneself because what we write comes from deep within ourselves. Tom may have left the human race, but he meets us again through his many works. That is what we can expect from a retreat with Father Louis.

His books are easy to read, their style is pleasant, never overblown. He writes simply, because he was a simple man, that is, unified. He is warm, he wants to take us along with him. He believes in what he says and writes. He is, at times, perhaps a little naive, by decreasing the difficulty of the task at hand, but he does this because he loves his reader. He writes so that the reader may grow, to show him his seriousness as a man and as a son of God. He wants to reveal to the reader what God calls him to, to invite him to an inner life, the true source of wisdom. That is the secret of Thomas Merton's influence.

Merton had a message to send to the world. He considered everything from his viewpoint as a monk. That was his domain and his strength. His domain because, in the Church or in society, there is not only monastic life; his strength because he was a man with only one goal, with only one battle: union with God and communion with humankind.

Solitude, from this perspective, becomes the symbol of this ultimate meeting and is sufficient for God and humankind. In a world that revolves around activism, mechanization, efficiency, stress, and speed, he will become the man of unity and peace by leading us to the center, to this Love, to this God whom he met through Jesus Christ, through the gift of the Holy Spirit.

Merton did not avoid certain exaggerations, inaccuracies, and errors. Perhaps he wrote too much? At times, we would have liked more conciseness, more depth, but Tom was the man that Christianity needed in a time of transition that didn't begin with Vatican II, but at the end of the Second World War.

Does the contemplative life have a role to play in the real world and if so, what is it? Father Louis, in all of his books, showed that the search for contemplation was an active service in response to God, integrating itself in the Christian community, and even more, that it is useful to all humankind. Like his brothers, he battles to face an existence that is restless, confusing, tiring, passionate, and deceptive. But this life of prayer is possible in the world.

> The exact worth which attracts the Christian to the desert and solitude is the profound feeling that God is enough. That is the very heart of monasticism.
>
> *Thomas Merton,* Silence in Heaven

> The monastic vocation is a vocation where one searches implicitly, if not explicitly, the experience of the union with God.
>
> *Thomas Merton,* Silence in Heaven

It is sufficient to have an authentic desire for God and what layperson, truly seeking God, doesn't have it?

Even more, he touched the lives of many who were indifferent or unbelieving. That is what brought him to be asked to contribute to the message of the contemplative monks at a bishop's synod held in 1967—a message seen as a "contemplative prayer for the world."

He had a great appetite for the absolute, for authenticity, a refusal of inertia, the deliberate will to shatter outdated rules to pieces...but like John of the Cross, the mystique will not eliminate the artist.

This simple man, this unusual Cistercian, was one of the most humane and engaging spiritual figures of this century. He was a man of paradoxes: of words and silence, a contemplative involved in the fight against racism, nuclear arms, the war in Vietnam; a man of solitude and of communication; a hermit who received many letters and visitors but by keeping himself in the background, he sought to deepen the fundamental human experience. He believed that the ultimate level of communication was communion, that we must become what we have already been (in our prototype, Eph 1:4–5, 11–12).

His vocation was inner unity. His message: the importance of the contemplative life by carrying the conflicts of the world in his heart.

He was a fervent religious who totally gave himself up to his monastic life. He was certainly one of the most prolific Cistercian authors. The Thomas Merton Studies Center at Bellarmine College in Louisville, Kentucky, holds a number of his unpublished works, manuscripts, and letters.

His teachings are drawn from classic monastic spirituality. His originality rests in the personal expression of feelings he gave them. He unites the traditional with the modern, a certain transparency with depth, theology with experience, the concrete. One word sums it up: contemplation. He is of the opinion that ordained monastic life transforms the monk into an authentic son of God, which is also true for all Christians devoted to a life of prayer; through contemplation, by steering us to the discovery of our true self (Gal 2:20). For him, the Christian of today's greatest need is inner truth, nourished by the contemplative spirit.

# Introduction

HUMAN EXISTENCE has no meaning for the atheist. No key turns in the lock. Christ, himself, came to bring the key which opens it, even more than that, he is the master key that works and resolves all problems. Through his conversion, Merton discovered the meaning of his existence.

To accomplish that, one must work to reconcile his sense of self with God, humankind, and the world: a unified life! Merton is a searcher for inner unity.

He also discovered, when he entered the American Trappists, that God loved him. To believe that we are loved, that is to say that God changes death into life, and that we live for someone else. Christ didn't only bring us one vision of the world, a reconciled existence—that is already a great deal—but also he offered the marvelous discovery and the transforming meeting of love.

Like the story of Zacchaeus which Saint Luke tells us (19:1–10), knowing that Christ was going to pass his way, this chief tax collector ran ahead and climbed a sycamore tree, because he was short in stature, to see who Jesus was.

Tom Merton wasn't very tall either; he ran by the monastic route and climbed his own tree, also wanting to see Jesus. If God loved the man of sin who is Zacchaeus/Merton, it is because God is not distant or indifferent. No, God was the one who saw him, loved him, and said: Zacchaeus, hurry and come down; for I must stay at your house today; I ask you to come down into your inner being.

Zacchaeus/Merton seen, recognized, loved by God.

What a meeting! What happiness!

The Lord received in the sinner's home, actually inviting himself into his house, welcomed in his home, that is to say, into his heart, into his interior self.

What a surprise! What honor!

At once, spare no expense!

What a bargain! What a celebration! What sharing! Christ enters the life of Zacchaeus, and Zacchaeus enters the life of Christ and it is a closeness.

Oh, he didn't lose any time that day! "Today salvation has come to this house, because he too is a son of Abraham" (Lk 19:9).

We hope that the reader will not regret his fifteen days of retreat by following Thomas Merton step by step.

But if God loved Zacchaeus, Zacchaeus must love God in return, giving love for love: "Look, half of my possessions, Lord, I will give to the poor," said Zacchaeus.

We have many treasures to discover which may be found in Thomas Merton's "fields." Surely, one must suffer a little, work the ground with a shovel and a pick, that is to say, slowly, but we will quickly find a few gold nuggets which will show us that we are digging in the right spot to find the treasure contained in the field: a union with God.

In order to do this, we must take the same steps as the spiritual master, know to get help for ourselves from those who have made the climb, and accept being accompanied.

These are areas where we do not venture ourselves as guides, but we are always rewarded with a contact with the beings of light, the enlightened beings, like Thomas Merton.

In this book, we embark on a fifteen-day retreat, with the aid and spiritual guidance of Thomas Merton through the use of his many published works. Our journey will be an effort to help each one of us reach our inner self. The chapters will proceed as follows:

1. Day One—A Conflicted Being
2. Day Two—A Convert
3. Day Three—A Chosen One
4. Day Four—A Monk
5. Day Five—A Hagiographer
6. Day Six—A Singer of Psalms
7. Day Seven—A Poet
8. Day Eight—A Protester
9. Day Nine—A Meditator
10. Day Ten—A Spiritual Master
11. Day Eleven—A Precursor of Interreligious Dialogue
12. Day Twelve—A Pioneer of Intermonastic Dialogue
13. Day Thirteen—A Mystic
14. Day Fourteen—An Apostle of Contemplation
15. Day Fifteen—A Traveling Companion

15 Days of Prayer
With Thomas Merton

# A Conflicted Being

## FOCUS POINT

At one time or another we all feel pulled and torn. It may be a feeling that we are spending too much time at work and not enough time with family. Perhaps it may be a feeling that goes beyond responsibility; for example, we may feel a need to develop our artistic self but we just don't seem to be able to "find the necessary time." Whatever the pull, it is the experience of being conflicted, the unsettled and restless self, and it is in conflict with that part of ourselves which desires harmony and peace.

*Writing is a component of my spiritual life.*
Thomas Merton, Letter to Dom Winandy,<br>August 30, 1955

Before following Merton through his life, his conversion, and his works, let us look at the hidden part of his being on which grace will act. By the words "hidden part of a being," we mean his resources, the original element that one discovers at the depths, that which reveals itself underneath.

There was a conflict inside Thomas Merton—and even many conflicts—that he knew to integrate, to overtake by his search for the absolute, to resolve by apostolic fruitfulness.

All and nothing: we detect a tragic contradiction, a drama. Impassioned by the absolute, he carried the conviction, deep within himself, of the uselessness of the human effort and the impossibility of authentic language which would be a reflection of God. That would explain his admiration for Ernest Hemingway's book *The Old Man and the Sea* and for Brice Parain's book *The Death of Jean Madec*.

Only God alone could totally satisfy his desires, the completeness of the being that he sought. His whole personality brought him to believe that the absolute and the relative, the all and the nothing, could only be irreconcilable. He lived in a conflicting situation.

It was from the time of his entering the Trappists that he could begin to hope for a certain harmony, thanks to the Rule of Saint Benedict, because it placed his concrete life in agreement with his deep conviction: God's absolute. In time, he would find all that he had definitively given up on at another level. The love of Christ fulfilled his need for affection and for the absolute. Let us not forget that, at the end of his life, the patriarch of monks—Saint Benedict—of whom Merton is the spiritual son, had a vision of the world in God.

Another conflict: monk and writer. To write is to communicate and, to a Christian, it is to be an apostle. Perhaps you may know of the whimsical statement of one of Merton's friends, Dom Jean Leclercq, a Benedictine monk of the Clervaux abbey.[1] He asked Merton: "Why do monks write?" Merton answered, "Because they don't speak."

Under the influence of his father, Merton should have been a painter, not a writer. How can we explain this line of progress for his creative energy? Was it a reaction against his family situation? Was it a lack of training in the techniques of painting and sketching? That scenario is more likely. In fact, it was that Merton could not create without an artistic apprenticeship, and as independent and solitary as he was, writing was a more obvious choice than painting.

One of the things that drove Saint Bernard to totally plunge himself into the solitude of Cîteaux seems to have been the will to escape literary ambition. Whereas, without having sought it, he became one of the greatest Latin authors of the Middle Ages. Considering this side of his personality, doesn't Merton resemble him a little?

Yet another conflict: he was Trappist, yet he felt the need to be a Carthusian. Contact was made with the Carthusians in Parkminster, England. In a letter addressed to Merton, they did not seem to hesitate in declaring that *infused* contemplation is the normal end of the contemplative vocation. And Father Louis (Merton) made this comment:

> The contemplative life is not just a complex system
> of exercises which the monks go through in order to
> pile up merits. God has brought us to the monastery
> to reveal himself to us, although it may only be in a
> very intangible and obscure way.
>
> The Sign of Jonas

In fact, he would be plagued all his life by the desire for a greater solitude so he would be able to approach God even more. (See *The Sign of Jonas* for Merton's further comments on this subject.)

Dom Porion, a Carthusian, then bursar for the order in Rome, wrote to Merton about his views:

> Most people find their balance in doing, in creating something; mere contemplative life requires a special grace—and a special fidelity. It requires a ripeness too, a maturity of soul which is not often to be met with in converts. This seems to result at least from the experiments we have made. But "to contemplate" in the first meaning of the word; to look directly at God and keep quiet—calm and purity being at once the condition and consequence of the vision—this indeed seems to me the true life, the life everlasting we are made for.
>
> *Dom Porion as quoted in* The Sign of Jonas

It was only little by little that Merton understood that the desire to be a Carthusian was infused by God in his heart, not to take him to the point of asking to go to another order, but to interiorize it there, where he was, to allow him to have a greater union with God and to have his books radiate this enlightenment. If this were not true, he would have been carried away by diversions: letters, visits, solicitations for this or that conference, and so on.

In spite of his experience as a hermit—for three years at the end of his life—Merton would never find appeasement for his desire for solitude. It must be mentioned that he played classical music records almost constantly, which irritated the other hermits who came to visit him, and who reminded him of the importance of absolute silence! And even more, he was totally incapable of being self-sufficient in terms of material things; he didn't even know how to cook. He had to face great numbers of letters and that was in no way compatible with the life of a hermit!

Perhaps he was not conscious enough that with the desire for solitude as a cenobite (a monk living under the Rule, under an abbot, and following a communal life), the soul must often listen only upon an invitation from the Holy Spirit to a more total withdrawal in the very framework of his initial vocation. That was exactly the normal response that Carthusians gave to other monks who were drawn by their lifestyle. And by their interiorization, their hermitic lifestyle, if that is the will of God, purifies itself and becomes fulfilling. The call to the desert is an exceptional vocation.

Every desire for solitude does not necessarily require a concrete action as a Carthusian. Merton did not sufficiently see that his discomfort and sufferings stemmed from this.

In fact, one must distinguish, among the desires infused by God, between those which God wants fulfilled, and those he does not want to be fulfilled but which are given to the soul to help it progress in the divine union, to free it, "to seek solitude for it," to spur it into action. Father Jean Surin, S.J., used to distinguish between the will of God and the movements of God.

Also, is the desire for solitude an infallible criteria for a Carthusian vocation? We must answer negatively. This desire cannot be isolated from a group of signs which constitute a vocation; but this desire will play a mystical role, the union with God.

These desires affect a great deal of good, even though we can't act upon them, not by our fault, but because God doesn't want us to act upon them. They produce a great fervor of spirit and heart, a perfect abandonment, a languor of love, a great self-abandonment. They produce more good in our souls than if, with divine grace, we had carried out these desires.

*Venerable François Marie Libermann (1802–1852)*

Merton did not perceive this delicate problem of spiritual direction. He resolved it by asking to live as a hermit. In fact, as we have said, his solitude was very mitigated. Add to this the conflict between God and the world, nature and grace, the flesh and the spirit (Rom 7:14–19), and we will have closed in a little on the complexity of Merton's personality. In fact, it was his "inner monk" that allowed him to achieve a certain unity, as his inner struggle, conflicts, and contradictions were reconciled, pacified, little by little.

## REFLECTION QUESTIONS

Is there a power, a strength of character, that may be discovered in that part of my life that seems to be in conflict? In my prayer, can I freely communicate not only my strengths, my hopes, and my dreams, but also my struggles and those areas of my life that are not at peace?

## DAY TWO
# A Convert

It may be a mistake to believe that there is nothing within that is in need of radical change and a new direction. The experience of conversion is not limited to the experience of moving from one faith stance in life to another, the external understanding of "being a convert." In a very real sense all people are converts because all people are called to change.

In *The Seven Storey Mountain*, Thomas Merton records these words spoken to him by Christ.

*I will lead you into solitude. I will lead you by the way that you cannot possibly understand, because I want it to be the quickest way.*

*I shall lead you into the high places of my joy and you shall die in Me and find all things in My mercy which has created you for this end and brought you from Prades to Bermuda to Saint Antonin to Oakham to London to Cambridge to Rome to New York to Columbia to Corpus Christi to Saint Bonaventure to the Cistercian Abbey of the poor men who labor in Gethsemani: That you may become the brother of God and learn to know the Christ of the burnt men.*

As recorded by Thomas Merton in
*The Seven Storey Mountain*

T homas Merton was born in Prades, France, located in the Pyrenees Mountains, on January 31, 1915. His father, a New Zealander, was a landscape painter and his mother was an American. His parents then settled down in France.

He attended school in France and in the United States. He lost his mother at the age of six and his father at the age of eighteen. His Grandfather oversaw his education. His Grandmother taught him his prayers, including the Our Father, which he would never forget. When he was studying at Cambridge, he traveled to Genoa, Rome, and Florence. It was in the churches in these Italian cities that he had his first contact with the sacred.

Upon his return to the United States, Merton studied at Columbia University in New York City. Curious about everything, he read a great deal, in particular French literature. One day, in the front window of a book store on Fifth Avenue, he saw the book entitled *Spirit of Medieval Philosophy* by Étienne Gilson, which he quickly bought. It made him think a great deal. Then he met with a Hindu monk who made him promise to read books on Christian mystics. In September 1938, after having devoured a book of correspondence between John Cardinal Newman and the Jesuit poet Gerard Manley Hopkins (1844–1889), he entered Corpus Christi Church in New York and requested to be baptized, which he was, on November 16 of that same year. During this period of his life he also wrote many poems and articles.

Drawn by Saint Francis of Assisi, Merton paradoxically decided to go on a retreat with the Trappists in Gethsemani, Kentucky. After having devoted himself to helping the African-Americans in Harlem and to teaching for a time, he requested the Cistercian habit at their monastery on December 10, 1941. He was twenty-six years old.

In 1942, he pronounced his first vows; he was ordained a priest in 1949. At the time of his solemn profession, which was before his ordination, he then became known as Father Louis. From then on, he dedicated his life to prayer, contemplation, and his mission as a writer. He became Master of Novices, and grew more and more attached to his monastic vocation. In doing so, he became a much loved spiritual father.

In 1948, he wrote his autobiography, published under the title, *The Seven Storey Mountain*, which became a bestseller. It was translated into many languages. Nicknamed, with certain emphasis, "the new Saint Augustine," his publications exerted such an influence that he was thought of as a type of twentieth-century Saint Bernard.

As much as *The Secular Journal of Thomas Merton*, published before his entry into the Trappists, is one of his weaker books, his book *The Seven Storey Mountain* is among his best, if not the best. This autobiography is easily read and does not lack depth. It must be noted that we now know better that Paul Claudel and many other converts went through identical steps of conversion, and that the meeting on the road to Damascus had been preceded by a few preliminaries. Under the influence of the Holy Spirit, conversion is more a ripening of the inner self, a work of the deepening of one's self, rather than an external incident.

For example, when God touched Paul Claudel, author of *Golden Head*, at Notre Dame Cathedral, at vespers on Christmas Day, 1886, he touched him at the very source of his being, the center of his soul and not at other points, such as his compassion, intelligence, will, memory, and so on. The proof of this is that, during the years that followed, Claudel had a mistress, who was the heroine of the book *Break at Noon*. Christ's climb up in Claudel was, then, a progressive one, as it was in Merton, as it is in all of us; it was done with many battles, difficulties, and falls.

What makes *The Seven Storey Mountain* so valuable is its sincerity, which we can compare, to a degree, with that of Saint Augustine's *Confessions*.


## GOD IN THE REARVIEW MIRROR

Merton shows admirably that on the route to Emmaus, an Other joined him, an Other whom he did not know. He walked the route with Him, and guided Merton without him knowing it, along the road which was full of rocks and ruts, this route which was his life, and ours. His reading of the Bible gave him the desire for the Eucharist, as in the story of the disciples on the evening of Easter, told by Saint Luke (24:13–35). We follow Merton along his slow, dry route where nothing is lit, then the small light grows and warms his heart. Christ hides, he only revealed himself externally, to the eyes of the apostles, what was going on inside them, to be seen by the eyes of their heart: they doubted. This doubt prevented them from seeing. To repeat one of Newman's expressions, they went from: "seeing and not knowing (on the road) to knowing and not seeing (at the inn in Emmaus)."

It is only later, like Merton, that we can discern his presence. Along the road of our own life, events occur which cause us either pain or pleasure. We don't see the hand of God in any of them. We don't figure out why they are happening or what significance they hold for us. We see them later as a reward for our obscure faith.

Look deeply at the event and you will see Jesus appear. At the time when it happened we don't have the mind-set to see his presence. It is only afterwards that we realize he guided our steps. Also, "in the present, it is God who hides himself; in the past, it is God who lets himself be seen."

God works in the spiritual desire. But the first desires are often veiled, that is, not said. Jesus leads to the discovery of this hidden desire and carries it to his conclusion by bypassing the initial desire.

Let us try to find that thread, which is even finer than a strand of hair, which passes through our lives, from our birth to today, which guides, joins, and explains it all: Christ, who walks alongside us on our route.

Often, it is a meeting which determines our destiny, an event that is insignificant to others, but not to us. When Augustine accepted the job as the teacher of rhetoric in Milan, he didn't think that he would meet the bishop of that city—Saint Ambrose—who would have a decisive influence over him. But when a person has faith in God, he will never miss having this sign in his life which is for him

alone, and only he is able to recognize it. The little events—
a meeting along the road—could have great consequences,
could be the cause of great enrichment. Perhaps they could
even reveal our destiny to us!

That meeting is enough to change a life so that it has
meaning, so that it has a precise direction, so that it would
truly be filled. How can we deny that our life is steered by a
golden thread?

Thomas Merton knew how to describe this, but he was
often a little long-winded. Edith Stein (a Carmelite who died
at Auschwitz and was canonized by Pope John Paul II in
1998) wrote about this in fewer words:

> When I think back on my life, across the years, I
> discover that it was very much a conversation which
> had a decisive influence within me. Then I formu-
> lated the thought that it was perhaps because of
> that—this conversation—that I should have gone to
> this city. What was not in my plan was in God's
> plan. And the more that similar events happen to
> me, the more alive becomes my conviction that my
> life, even in its very details, possesses a perfect co-
> herence of meaning to the all-seeing eyes of God.
>
> *Edith Stein as quoted by M.A. Neyer*

## THE CONVERSION

If the soul turns toward the self, the soul is more, it is greater.
Also, it edifies and stabilizes itself in good.

If the soul turns away from the self, it suffers a loss of
the self, which makes it less. Then it falls into decay, leaning
toward nothingness.

The passage from a lesser self to a greater self is the process of conversion. It is the opposite of aversion or loathing. Aversion is made up of radical poverty of spirit, deep-seated inner poverty and suffering, hunger of the self, spiritual death. It has a nihilistic effect, due to a fault of nature, an injury to the soul, which comes from ignorance of the truth, when the truth is food for the soul.

We can see the drama in which Merton—the man—is engaged. On one hand, he is called toward the most high, the greater self. On the other hand, he is drawn toward the depths of nothingness or the lesser self. In the first case, he works to reach the area of similarity with God. In the second case, he works to reach the area of dissimilarity with God. In this area of dissimilarity, the soul is capable of making the choice of inferior spiritual values, and, thus, is carried by the course of events toward the depths of nothingness. By turning away from God, not only do we abandon the road which leads to the end for which the self is created, but we turn away from our very own true self. Thomas Merton makes us pay attention to this reorientation through Christ toward the ultimate end: the One, our God.

Merton does not dramatize this situation; he treats it with good sense and humor. It remains true that this conversion is an upheaval of his freewheeling ways which were abandoned along with the abandonment of sin, by which he, under the influence of the Holy Spirit, was fully welcomed to the kingdom of God.

It is the same subject as before, but it has become different. That is what Merton presents to us in his autobiography. Is it the convert himself, or is it an image of the convert that comes into play? Is it a miracle, or is it a respectful confluence of secondary causes that are used by God? By which route can conversion be registered in the psyche? These are some of the many questions which come to our minds when we read *The Seven Storey Mountain.*

## REFLECTION QUESTIONS

When have I been surprised by God? What were the circumstances of the events and the experiences of life that have invited me to think and respond in a new way? Are any of those same kind of events and experiences at work in my life today? Am I being called to something more?

## DAY THREE
# A Chosen One

### FOCUS POINT

Do I believe that God has a preference for me, that in some way God has called me and I have responded to that call? Do I believe that God is in relationship with me and desires to be an integral part of my life or do I believe that such a relationship is reserved for a chosen few? Do I understand my response to God's call as vocation?

*The man who loses this sense of his own personal destiny, and who renounces all hope of having any kind of vocation in life has lost all hope of happiness.*

Thomas Merton, *No Man Is an Island*

*If you believe you know what your vocation is, then you
have none.*

Thomas Merton to his novices, cited by Bruno Ronfard in
*Thomas Merton: moione et ecrivain.*

———

The two texts at the beginning of this chapter concern
the subject of vocation—a topic that is often discussed
throughout Merton's works. The second text at the beginning of this chapter is a sort of soapbox or Zen conundrum.
It identifies a quest which is never fulfilled and manifests a
certain pleasure in confusing, in the same manner as do Zen
monks who would like to destroy the too-rational framework of their questioners.

Vocation is a central theme in Merton's work. That is
why we must, above all, begin to examine it, beginning with
his book, *No Man is an Island* which was first published in
1955.

By virtue of the universal call for redemption, each of
us goes through life with a divine vocation, but on the route
of divine vocation, each one of us must walk in his or her
own way. The apostle teaches us that the Spirit of God dis-
tributes a certain number of gifts to humankind—here, we
must reread 1 Corinthians 12:1–31—and he adds, by these
same gifts, the Spirit assigns each of us a place and a specific function in the ecclesiastical body, just as the limbs are
part of the whole body. Each of these gifts is a vocation
from God. It is this vocation that, by paying attention to
it, all humans must try to discern and illuminate in themselves.

Our vocation from God does not remain static at a degree of nondifferentiated universality. It refines itself to the point of becoming individually specific, and it is here that variableness and ambiguity intervene. That is why and when we must pay specific and particular attention.

It is for every baptized person to discover if they have a vocation and how to respond to the love of God. The vocation will be the means for ensuring that God is always first and, through this means, God will signify to each person that he or she must respond to his love and how. Our response to this love from God is limited by time as much as by the chosen means. We must realize what God's plans are for us, even for all eternity. It would be good at this point to read Ephesians 1:1–14.

But it is also correct to say that when I find my vocation, then God will truly become my God, because from then on God has entered into my very existence. He stops being a distraction in order to become a concrete reality, that is to say, the living Being who is loved. Then God will become real in each person, and with and through God, everything else will become real as well.

When we discover our vocation, we discover a deeper level of our inner self. We recreate our self and build it up. To carry out that vocation is to actualize ourselves, and to actualize ourselves is to fulfill our life. As soon as each person begins to enter into his or her true vocation, it seems as if God is alongside, with watchful eye, caring for the one who has answered the call.

The committed person is filled with confidence and joy. He or she loses the feeling of being abandoned and is delivered from doubt and anguish through association with creation, through which is found meaning and significance arising out of a story that is both individual and collective at the same time. Each and every discovery of vocation is truly an annunciation.

A vocation is like a seed germinating. All that is lived, both good and bad, finds itself recuperated and purified because a vocation is a dynamism that affects a synthesis in our inner self. We could define it as the existential impossibility to give another meaning to our life.

Paul Valéry says, "Man is born with many facets: his life is successful if he dies unified." Dispersion and distraction provide obstacles to a vocation, a straying from the target, that would make the search for unity fail.

We all know the adage: What is a great life if it isn't thoughts of youthfulness carried out by the mature? In a similar vein, we may exist; but with a vocation, we live. Vocation is a constructive dynamism that transforms everything.

At the age of twenty, we have many vocations and various abilities. A young person is characterized by a sense of determination. To become an adult, a person must make a clear choice. Not to choose would mean that nothing would happen. But by making a choice, a person may feel that limitations have set in and personal worth is diminished.

In fact, our existence forces us to make the choice of a single stream, a single road. But the art of living consists precisely in rejecting from the milieu around that chosen stream or road, those secondary vocations which we have set aside so that we may give all of ourselves to the primary one. There are, however, secondary vocations, discovered in the heart of the primary vocation, which give it all its brightness.

There is no one vocation which does not bring another higher one, often unexpressed, along with it, but in which we find a springboard. The primary vocation is really only a means to build our many selves. Here, we must go and read the parable of the Talents in Matthew 25:14–30.

A vocation is born by using circumstances, chance (luck is really God's logic), and events (the masters that God gives us). That which is revealed to us first, perceived as something new, is often seen in time as a deepening of what we unknowingly already possess.

A vocation comes to us from deep within ourselves, and we may feel passed over or bypassed. It allows us to discover who we are and our place in the world and in history. With the fragments of our inner self, of our life, it assembles the puzzle that we are. At the heart of our own vocation, we evolve to be more of the same.

> The search for what God wants here and now is made on the basis of our own initiative, our likes, our insight, our determination....What God wants us to do is what is most in agreement with his design. It is for us to elaborate on this harmony, progressively as we better understand the link to established between our present behavior and God's design for us. This work of perception inevitably brings certain imperfections with it. We do not have any certainty. All we know is that our submissiveness to the Holy Spirit and the seriousness of our search allow us to reach God's desire to the closest degree as we are able.
>
> *Father Gouvernaire, S.J., in "Saint Paul's Perception,"*
> Christian Life, *no. 193, 1976*

There are few persons who could say what Gabriel Marcel did in his book *Conversations With Father Boutang*: "I have the feeling that I have almost fulfilled my vocation. On the whole, it seems to me that I have done just about what I sought to do."

Many have come close to their true vocation but missed it. Why? Misdirected freedom? Not listening to our inner self? A break away from grace? Those near-misses are a big mystery—from which stems the necessity keeping our spiritual attention alert to discovering, living, and fulfilling our vocation as one of the baptized.

Silence is a way that permits us to deeply grasp the meaning of our inner self. Also, for the person who wants to grasp God's vocational plan, silence becomes a necessity. Stillness and quiet are like nourishment, because it is through these that the presence of the Holy Spirit can be attended to and interior happenings inside, through, and around can be perceived.

At the beginning, there is an awakening, a spark which expresses the self. At the finish, there is often a separation, at times immense, between where we wanted to be, what we wanted to do, and what life has been made by using the debris of our wishes. There have been errors in our itinerary, and we find ourselves quite far from the connection. We have relied more upon human means than upon God. "Growing old," wrote François Mauriac, "how difficult it is to remain faithful to the young men we were."

After all, set formulas never explain what the call is or what our response should be. Those who hear the call can do nothing but live it. Their life is the response, more or less accomplished, to that call.

A vocation? That is something which is infinitely mysterious. It is God's secret in each of our souls, a gigantic secret. The story of Yahweh questioning Samuel is a story where it is said that the young man Samuel asked Eli three times about the importance of a certain call that came during the night. When Eli finally realized that it was the Lord, Eli instructed Samuel in this manner: "Go, lie down; and if he calls you, you shall say, 'Speak, LORD, for your servant is listening.'"

At even first glance, this story makes us see that a vocation is a seed of love. Who could doubt that a vocation is the slow growing of a seed—a growing which involves a whole lifetime, with its choices, uncertain beginnings, its hesitations and problems, its passages from an ordinary quality to a higher one, its phases of crisis and peace, its changing moods of the heart, and, finally, its ultimate consummation? Who could doubt that a vocation is the story of a person who grows in reality only when God becomes real in him, and that this gift-of-God vocation is everything?

Each believer should be able to say to Christ who calls to him—no matter what means is chosen to follow him: marriage, consecrated celibacy, or other routes—

- By your Word, you have acted in me, all the while remaining hidden to my eyes which have been veiled by false light;
- By your Word, you have thrown a grain of love into my heart which grew, even before I knew about it. As a result, we have met. You have entered my life, have interrupted my existence;
- By your Word, you have given different weights to all my worldly values so that I can be born into a greater love;

- By your Word, you have given me a glimpse of
  your face and revealed that you are more than
  just a name, an idea, that you are a living and
  loved person who gives of himself, then disap-
  pears, who shows himself and then flees, but who
  makes us dig deeper in our desire to possess you.

In short, a Christian vocation is a seed of love, planted
inside us by the Word of God. It is a concrete attitude: just
like Samuel's.

A vocation is both a call and an answer. In his *Asian
Journal*, Merton copies a few lines from the poet Pierre
Emmanuel and then notes:

To conceive a call of God as an expressed order to
carry out a task certainly is not always false, but it
is only true after a long interior struggle in which it
becomes obvious that no such constraint is apparent. It also happens that the order comes to maturity along with the one who must carry it out and
that it becomes in some way this very being, who
has now arrived at full maturity. Finally, the process
of maturing can be a mysterious way of dying, provided that with death the task begins.

*Thomas Merton*, Asian Journal

We should have the desire to reflect upon our vocation
as baptized members of the Church, on our involvement in
the Church, as part of the Body of Christ. If these actions
are carried out, then God will all the more often reveal himself to us in the gift of our vocation; but this revelation will
only come progressively.

## REFLECTION QUESTIONS

Have I made a clear choice in my life, a choice that I now understand as a response to the call of God and my cooperation with the power of grace? Can I bring the experiences of my vocation to the Lord in prayer? When I reflect on my vocation do I do so with a grateful heart or is there something that may be incomplete, untested, or not yet clear?

# A Monk

## FOCUS POINT

A monk may live in a monastery but not all who live in a monastery are monks. It is possible to answer the call of the monastery bell, to follow all of the rules, to embrace all of the externals, and never internalize and embrace the experience as a necessary way of living. To be a monk is more than the physical experience of being, it is a core experience of life, it is a way of seeing, it is a chosen way to interpret life and to respond to life.

*This inner "I," who is always alone, is always universal: for in this inmost "I," my own solitude meets the solitude of every other man and the solitude of God. Hence it is beyond division, beyond limitation, beyond selfish affirmation. It is only this inmost and solitary "I" that truly loves with the love and the spirit of Christ. This "I" is*

*Christ Himself, living in us: and we, in Him, living in the Father.*

Thomas Merton, *Disputed Questions*

P seudo-Dionysius, that friendly unknown from the fifth
century, wrote, in Chapter 6 of his book, *The Ecclesiastical Hierarchy*:

> Monks are called in this way because they practice
> the cult in a manner that is pure, that is to say, in
> service to God. And also because their lives, far from
> being divided, remain perfectly unified because they
> have united themselves together by a holy contem-
> plation which excludes all distractions, in a manner
> that leads them towards a way of living that is true
> to God and also towards the perfection of divine love.

Pseudo-Dionysius' definition, as given above, is among
one of the most perfect that we could encounter.

Raimundo Panikkar's reflections concerning the monk
as a universal model recalls Merton's excellent text in his
chapter on solitude in *Disputed Questions*.

Both of these quotes show that the person who is aware
of the spiritual dimension looks to concentrate on the search
for the inner center of his being. The objective is to be able
to center oneself and the universe on the supreme truth.

In these days, when many people live in, but do not
withstand very well, the experience of solitude (often a solitude that they have not chosen for themselves), Merton's
reflections could help them develop their deepest inner self.

When a person is overtaken by overpowering relationships, or aimed toward immediate gratification, he or she often falls short of the ultimate self, where, at times, a feeling of uneasiness develops that may pave the way to depression. Well-ordered solitude allows a person to return to the source of living water and to find, in some cases, a true spiritual blossoming.

For Panikkar, the monk is an example of a person who aspires, with all of his being, to reach the ultimate goal in life by renouncing all that is not essential, so that he may concentrate only on this single and unique goal. In this description, we can see a model of human life that has a constituent dimension of solitude because each person has, in his or her own being, a point, even in marriage, where solitude is inevitable.

For Merton, a monk is a person who has been called by the Holy Spirit to forego the usual preoccupations, desires, and ambitions of other human beings so that he can consecrate his life to a search for God. The monk is a man of God. Therefore, given that all people have been created by God for the purpose of being able to find God, they are all, in a certain way, rightly called to be "people of God," even if they aren't all called to be monks in a monastery. Each of them, however, must truly seek God, not seek souls for God, but seek God himself.

Merton studied the different forms of monastic life: that of the Benedictines, Cistercians, Carthusians, and so on, and shows the common denominator: solitude for God. He wrote in his book *The Silent Life* that the "monastic vocation is, by its very nature, a call to solitude." We do not adopt solitude just to be able to pray better, we adopt solitude to seek union with God himself.

The reflections of Merton, as a monk, are beneficial because many people experience the richness of a life that revolves around God, but they do not know or cannot live it truly without concrete direction from a spiritual guide who would help them. And even more lay people, especially those who frequent monasteries—and they are becoming more and more numerous today—or Christians engaged in apostolic duties feel the need for an exclusive spiritual renewal centered on God alone. One does not have to be a monk or live in poverty, but we need to discover the richness of a life of solitude, filled with God, even if it is only for a few weekends. Thomas Merton can help these seekers because he has the charisma to be able to speak about the interior life, about the contemplative life, and about its effects on the world.

When we make a reference to the greatness of the monastic ideal and to the excellence of living this way, we don't want to, in any way, give the impression that monastic orders are, by their very nature, superior to other religious orders, but Merton wanted to show the benefits that they can bring into the lives of certain lay people and perhaps, if we should also believe Panikkar, to all humankind.

Françiose Dolto has also joined in this idea (in her book entitled *Solitude*) of reintroducing solitude to the lives of her contemporaries. Like Merton, she has underlined the positive aspect, as much for psychological equilibrium as for creativity. Both writers have shown the possibilities of spiritual renewal and the validation that it brings, an interior life being the necessary route for every spiritual progression. As a result, the practice of solitude brings truer relationships; only those who have withstood the trial of solitude can truly say: "us." Alas, not everyone knows how to make the best use of solitude.

One must even recognize that solitude brings certain dangers with it, that is has certain disheartening aspects. It is not recommended for those whose characters dictate a need for relationships, for those who are fond of discussions, and for those who cannot live without social contacts. But, even so, any conquest of one's self, done in truthfulness and with clearheadedness, brings with it some aspects or parts of solitude.

## REFLECTION QUESTIONS

When I journey to the "monastery of my inner self," do I find a place well kept and in order, or do I find a place ignored, abandoned, unused, nothing more than an empty shell? What do I need to choose to do today in order to reclaim my true self and to seek the life that has been offered to me as gift?

DAY FIVE

# A Hagiographer

A constant tradition in the practice of the spiritual life is to look to the lives of the saints. These men and women, who are more like ourselves than we might first imagine, can be a source of inspiration for us. When we spend time with the life of a saint we do not look for the extraordinary but rather for the ordinary. We do so because it is in the ordinary, made extraordinary by a life of faith, that we may discover practical nourishment for our spiritual journey.

*A saint is always a sign from God...a blank mirror on which God has projected some glints of his own divine love.*

Thomas Merton,
Preface to *Bernard of Clairvaux*

In the beginning of his monastic life, Thomas Merton tried to write about the lives of the saints. He thought that this particular style of literature would allow him to reconcile his vocation as a writer with his vocation as a monk. By purifying the source, by making his talent a tangible means for service to the Church, he hoped to be able to resolve his problem—how to be a monk and a writer—by bypassing it. In fact, we must recognize that the best of Merton was not to be found there. But through a contact with the saints, he converted himself and, as well, converted some of his readers.

In his book, *Last of the Fathers*, he retraced the admirable epic of Saint Bernard of Clairvaux and the Rancé reform (1626–1700), that is to say, the story of the Trappists and their conquest of America. This blossoming of the spiritual brothers of Saint Bernard, in the country which enjoys leadership in the technical world of today, is an important work in the history of monasticism of the Church.

*What Are These Wounds?* is the biography of a Cistercian sister who lived in the twelfth century, Saint Lutgarte of Aywières. He used this book as a forum to point out the essential aspects of Saint Bernard's spirituality. *Exile Ends in Glory* tells the story of the life of Mother Marie Berchmans (Marie Piguet), a Trappist missionary, who left an impression of saintliness in Japan at the beginning of this century.

In order to meet Jesus, we can benefit from and be helped by the experiences of these saints—these chosen people— who have been enlightened. We must not try to imitate them in a material way—because each soul has its own personal itinerary—but use their stories as a means to stimulate us.

In each human being, whether a criminal or saint, there is a place of darkness and a place of light. What the saints teach us is a way to reduce the areas of darkness so that the areas of light will shine through.

And then, this examination of the lives of saints will teach us about our inner self. "Tell me which Saints you like and I will tell you who you are" is an old saying. For the saints to which we are attracted become the projections of our deepest spiritual self, that is to say, the best of our inner self. And then, they will teach us who we seek to be and how we must go about it, so as to seek enlightenment. The light of God comes to us filtered through them. Through them, the light is more available. Through them, it is more tangible.

A pilgrim from Ars said, when speaking about Saint John Vianney: "I saw God in a man." To see a saint is to have a vision of the invisible. A saint is truly a mirror of the invisible. A saint is also a great lover because he or she took the exalted road, the path which surpasses all others, the road of charity (1 Cor 13:4–7).

A saint is also a being of light. Julien Green often wrote that when Jacques Maritain—who went to visit Merton in his hermitage—entered a room, it was as if a ray of sunshine had come into it. The shine of truth in the Thomist philosopher reached those who were in his presence. This spiritual glow makes us think of the following passage from the Gospel: "The eye is the lamp of the body. So, if your eye is healthy, your whole body will be full of light" (Mt 6:22).

Wherever a saint goes, a fire is lit. The words "I came to bring fire to the earth, and how I wish it were already kindled!" (Lk 12:49) come back to us to mean, in the words of Saint John of the Cross, "Where there is no love, put in love and you will harvest love."

A saint is a being who conforms to the will of God. In the spiritual life, everything plays a role in the union of will with God, that is to say, the desire that "thy will be done." But there is a big difference between saying it and doing it!

Thomas Merton showed us, in his studies of the saints' lives, just how much they were revelations of a living God who enters our lives, our daily lives. He knows God through experience which is, above all, a knowledge of his mercy. God's mercy is spread over us by the five wounds of Jesus Christ. These are the windows by which Bernard throws his glance toward the heavens. It is in this way that the "Doctor Mellifluus" helps us to come to complete fulfillment of the knowledge that enters us through the mystery of God. As it is written in Colossians:

I want their hearts to be encouraged and united in love, so that they may have all the riches of assured understanding and have the knowledge of God's mystery, that is, Christ himself, in whom are hidden all the treasures of wisdom and knowledge (2:2–3).

Finally, in this chapter devoted to reflection on the lives of the saints—especially Saint Bernard of Clairvaux—we are invited seek the enlightened and saintly beings for whom we have a particular affection, those with whom we have certain personal affinities. We must pray to them, but also examine how they may become channels of divine love for our daily lives. Some examples of saints that have already served as beacons for the faithful are as follows: Saint Vincent, Saint Thérèse of Lisieux, Saint Bernadette of

Lourdes, Saint Thomas Aquinas, and, why not, Saint Bernard of Clairvaux?

We must remember that Saint Bernard was born in Fontaine-lès-Dijon (France) in 1090, and died in Clairvaux in 1153. He was a monk at Cîteaux (in 1112), the cradle of the reformed Benedictines or Cistercians. He founded the Clairvaux Abbey (in 1115) and preached the Second Crusade. He was an adversary of Abelard's rationalism and a promoter of the devotion to the Blessed Virgin Mary; he was a counselor to kings and popes. A shining example of a monk and priest, Bernard was very active, writing a number of works, particularly a famous commentary on the Song of Songs. Saint Bernard has been declared a Doctor of the Church, an official guide so designated by the Church.

Thomas Merton was a great admirer of Saint Bernard. Toward the middle of this century, he contributed, to a large extent, to his rediscovery by the Cistercians and Trappists as well as by the general public. These two great influences would certainly have understood each other. Saint Bernard lived in Christ and Christ lived in him because, as Saint Bernard had come to understand, as illustrated by Chapter 7 of the Rule of Saint Benedict (which is followed by the Cistercians), that his nothingness was, in fact, greatness because it was Christ, not Bernard, who was the greatness in Bernard. The nothingness had discovered God. What are human beings, asked the Saint, if God doesn't reveal himself to them? This is also the question we must ask in our prayers.

## REFLECTION QUESTIONS

When I recall the story of my favorite saint, can I recall, in the retelling, something that can nourish or inspire me today? Does a person have to be officially canonized in order to be a saint, a source of inspiration for myself or for another? Are there qualities in me, or qualities that I desire to possess, that could be considered saintly? Do I then give praise and thanks to God for the power of grace working within me?

## DAY SIX
# A Singer of Psalms

### FOCUS POINT

"To you, O Lord, I lift of my soul" (Psalm 25). "As a deer longs for flowing streams, so my soul longs for you, O God" (Psalm 42). "I cry aloud to God, aloud to God, that he might hear me" (Psalm 77). "Sing joyfully to God our strength" (Psalm 81).

*The Psalms are the nourishment of the inner life and form the material of meditations and our own personal prayer, so that at last one comes to live them and experience them as if they were our own songs, our own prayers.*

Thomas Merton, *Bread in the Wilderness*

Thomas Merton faithfully celebrated the Divine Office (now called the Liturgy of the Hours) in his Abbey at Gethsemani. This official prayer of the Church is composed, in large part, of the psalms, religious poems which sum up all of the experiences in Israel. For centuries, they have been the basis of both Jewish and Christian liturgical prayer.

Often, the psalms are misunderstood on account of the curses and calls for vengeance which they contain. We must understand that these are in reference to the forces of evil which are at work in the world. But the psalms are also, and above all, hymns of praise. Merton wrote a marvelous little book called *Praying the Psalms*, which is one of the best modern introductions to the recitation of the Psalter by a Christian today.

Merton's autobiography, *The Seven Storey Mountain*, finishes with this sentence: "This book ends here, but not the quest." Merton pursued this quest mainly through and by means of the psalms: a quest of a human being for God. His personal transformation, by and through the monastic life, occurred in a way which was dictated by the second commandment, which is similar to the first: "Love your neighbor as yourself," from which comes the fight against all forms of alienation.

Merton also wanted to change the world and life itself. From the depths of his monk's cell, by disconcerting the pious, meeting with disapproval from his first readers who were shocked by such an opinion, he committed himself to both a spiritual and social battle. He lived this quest in his liturgical plan by and through the psalms. The Benedictine peace is not a status quo; it is not to not make waves. It is founded on a vision of human beings, who are the image of God and, therefore, capable of transcendence.

This capability for transcendence is why this committed monk wanted to raise such concerns. This solitary person is such because he was anxious to work toward the spiritual evolution of humanity. The psalms are a great means for him to embrace the universe, bring it before God, and assume it, through his life of prayer and penance.

One of the main themes of the psalms is the fight, the fight against a mysterious enemy—the enemy that at once transcends humanity and is within each of us. Tied to this theme of fight, and equally as important, is the theme of the manifestation of God through praise of him. Israel, in the height of battle, invoked Yahweh as its all-powerful help. Only he could derail the enemy. If the total existence of a monk is suspended in favor of a quest for God, God will certainly respond by helping us get rid of the obstacles which separate us from him, and which prevent us from approaching him.

In the servant psalms, Merton discovered Christ. In praying the psalms of the people of God, Merton repeated them with the whole Church. In the Messianic psalms, Merton saw, just beneath the surface, an anointed King of God, like another David, the one who would bring to an end this cosmic conflict, which now fills the pages of history now, and will do so up until the time when God is everything for everyone. In the historic psalms, Merton saw that his own history was the history of Israel.

In his poems which express his yearning for God, Merton helps us discover incomparable beauty. Their enlightenment and music fill Merton's soul. He poured his life into them, molding his most personal feelings by recapturing the verses that the intoned psalm offered him. This form of prayer—progressively as poverty dug into his heart—took possession of him and taught him the ways of true dialogue with the living God. It is for each of us to tune our voices to that of Jesus Christ, our Psalmist. It is for each of us to progressively discover, by our own prayer experience, what effective place can and should be held by the psalms in our lives. It is suitable to change the Psalmist's prayer into our personal prayer, to adapt it to our own needs, but it is, above all, the prayer of the entire Mystical Body. It reaches all humankind through its distress and through its praise of the Lord.

The disciples asked: "Lord, teach us how to pray," and Merton, along with the whole of the monastic tradition, offers us a Psalter. All themes are addressed within: the creation for us to praise it; the law for us to follow it; history for us to relive it; the Messiah for him to triumph; suffering, needs, enemies, anguish so that he will deliver us from it; and, finally, God, so that we can glorify him. It is a tangible prayer, Christ's prayer. It could never become ours because it was his. The Son of God who was made man carried all human weaknesses in his own flesh. It is he, the heart of all humankind, who sheds his blood here before God; it is he who takes our place and prays for us and through us.

The Christian who sings or reads the psalms fulfills them. Throughout the diverse experiences lived across the centuries, one single man—the head and the members—builds himself. That single entity of many constituents is Christ. He lives what all the members of the ecclesiastical body live. With them, he worries, fights, works, and, therefore, fulfills, giving meaning to history. The history of Israel, that is to say, the history of the people of God—the Church—is also in a certain measure the history of each soul. The psalms are the miraculous bread, prepared by Christ, to nourish those who followed him into the desert. As Merton says in *The Seven Storey Mountain:*

> By listening to the silence which bathes his heart, by marveling in the love of Christ, which he never saw but knows as well as he knows himself, the monk feels the secret presence of the Word blossom in him like a marvelous hidden smile.

The psalms reveal the true face of Christ, of God. That is precisely the reason that the book *Bread in the Wilderness* is subtitled *The Mystery of the Psalms*, that is to say, the mystery of Christ at work in the world.

## REFLECTION QUESTIONS

Have I discovered the power of the psalms and do I incorporate them into my daily prayer? Do I try to form the intention of joining my prayer with the prayer of the entire Church? Is there a particular psalm that is a source of comfort for me, or a source of hope, or a psalm that uniquely expresses praise and thanksgiving for me?

# DAY SEVEN
# A Poet

"If the poets' verse be fable, then is all your knowledge fable," exclaimed Columcille, of the Irish guild of poets. It is in poetry that the heart, indeed the soul, of a person is revealed. In the revelation of the heart, we may discover truth; and in the discovery of the truth, we may encounter the holy and touch something of the sacred.

*Sweet brother, if I do not sleep*
*My eyes are flowers for your tomb;*
*And if I cannot eat my bread,*
*My fasts shall live like willows where you died.*
*If in the heat I find no water for my thirst,*
*My thirst shall turn to springs for you, poor traveler.*

*Where, in what desolate and smokey country,*
*Lies your poor body, lost and dead?*

*And in what landscape of disaster*
*Has your unhappy spirit lost its road?*
*Come, in my labor find a resting place*
*And in my sorrows lay your head,*
*Or rather take my life and blood*
*And buy yourself a better bed—*
*Or take my breath and take my death*
*And buy yourself a better rest.*

*When all the men of war are shot*
*And flags have fallen into dust,*
*Your cross and mine shall tell men still*
*Christ died on each, for both of us.*

*For in the wreckage of your April Christ lies slain,*
*And Christ weeps in the ruins of my spring:*
*The money of Whose tears shall fall*
*Into your weak and friendless hand,*
*And buy you back to your own land:*
*The silence of Whose tears shall fall*
*Like bells upon your alien tomb.*
*Hear them and come: they call you home.*

*The Seven Storey Mountain*

———

This poem—chosen from among so many others—brings to the forefront the death of his brother, John Paul, a pilot, shot down in the North Sea during the Second World War. He had visited Merton at Gethsemani in the months preceding his departure for Europe. John Paul had been baptized in a neighboring parish and had made his first Communion at the monastery.

What was Thomas looking for in poetry?

Is not the greatness of poetry in what it says by not actually saying it? Is that not why, when two people read the same poem, they see something different? A certain reality transcends this one. That is why he spoke volumes by including what wasn't said, as if words were inadequate. Each of us reading a poem discovers something different, depending upon our own experiences, feelings, thought processes, or our own wanderings. If one is hurt by it, another may remain untouched.

The poet wants to crack open the words, he wants to invent others, and he is obligated to use only the language that is available to him, but, at times, with a surplus of feeling. That is why he destroys the ordinary significance of the spoken word so that he can force the birth of a new language which brings different and new meanings with it.

To speak the unspeakable—the sorrow felt at the death of his brother—without repeating it loudly so as to not change the mystery, that is the audacity of the poet! Whatever it is, he wants to communicate and what he wants to communicate—he knows it—is incommunicable. That is why—in spite of it all—he proceeds to use mere words, in an effort to say the unspeakable, which is always recaptured.

Also, a poem is never a conclusion, it is always a beginning, an attempt to say the words, and it should lead to silence. Poetry is a type of experience that is like death because poetic language throws itself at the unspeakable things of our reality. Poetry can do nothing but fail. It is a veiling and unveiling of our inner self. In this failure, in this non-progress and in this veiling hides the unsaid, which is invisible and which we must learn how to decipher. The unspeakable takes off and dies in the signs but reminds us, by that action, that it is beyond all signs.

We must throw ourselves beyond the inadequacy of words, to seek sounds not yet heard, and then the words will seek to respond to the demands of the musical nature of the poet's feelings. They are words, yet they aren't really words, because the poetic experience is preceded by passion, emotion, and, above all, pain and suffering.

Poetry changes the way we look at what we are, or at least it makes us begin to see inside our inner world, almost in the same way we see the external world. Poetry represents an image of the passing from real time to eternity because it suggests what will make it barely comprehensible; it suggests our relationship with the One who is found in the incomprehensible.

Poetic activity could perhaps be a spiritual experience. This is not a great certainty; the sacred goes much deeper and prayer opens us to a higher certainty. On the other hand, poetry brings us closer to our true feelings, to our true self, to our Source. Merton's poetry is poetry created in silence which leads us to our own silence.

## REFLECTION QUESTIONS

The poet carefully chooses each word, for nothing can be wasted or carelessly discarded. What word(s) resonated within you and called forth from within you a deeper response? Did you experience yourself being led to a sense of the other? Did you prayerfully acknowledge the presence of mystery and of the sacred? Did the poem produce for you a specific mood or reaction and were you able to take your response to prayer?

## DAY EIGHT

# A Protester

### FOCUS POINT

Each person of conscience or, if not of conscience, at least of expressed opinion, will occasionally come face to face with an event or experience that is beyond their control. So powerful, the event calls forth from you some sort of response, but you are unable to effect your desired action or change. At such a moment, a person might choose to act by announcing their protest. It is your judgment that you do not agree, that you are not pleased, that you hope for something better and something more. Protests are not always welcomed and often misunderstood. Protest is always an announcement, a proclamation of some felt truth or emotion, that an individual person determines is essential to their definition of who they are.

*A monk is essentially a person who adopts a critical attitude with respect to the world.*

Thomas Merton, *Asian Journal*

———

When he was a student, Thomas Merton became interested in politics. Some people said that he was very "leftist." Later, he was strongly critical of the contemporary world and of the structures in society. His contempt for the world was, on his part, an acceptance of the need for change. He rose up "against" the world in order to change it. Here, the word "world" is used in the Johannine sense, that is to say, where the forces that are opposed to the coming of the kingdom are at work, but not those of the cosmos, which are good, since they were created by God. He criticized Western society by recalling that the first monks had been protesters against the society of their time.

Did Merton really "see" that changes based solely on economic infrastructures simply aren't enough? The monk sought to change consciousness of human beings because that is what was polluted and confused.

Merton was a man who reached or was on the brink of reaching a certain realization. He dug deeply into the depths of his inner self and felt that he had broken through to the secret of freedom. His entrance into the monastic life provided him a communal life where each person gave of his talents and received in accordance with his needs. From that point, he extended this way of seeing things.

He denounced totalitarianism in all its forms. He denounced alienation in all its forms. For him, Christianity is the antidote for everything oppressive to humans. We will see him take the side of peace, nonviolence, enter into a debate on the question of racial inequality, protest the Vietnam war, deplore nuclear arms. By his visible public stance, Merton, a Trappist monk, created many newspaper headlines in the United States and elsewhere.

At times, his superiors feared for him and expressed certain reservations. Should Merton have stayed within the confines of the cloister? That isolation was the whole problem. For him, self-involvement was a matter of conscience, but he may not have seen that he was sometimes inadequately informed about the subjects on which he took a stand. Was he never told about this?

A monk living in seclusion could not be as aware of worldly things as a layperson. And, should a monk involve himself in the world when he has effectively left it? Did Tom have any training in the intricacies of the political fray? Add to that the fact that Merton's personality contained a good dose of innocence along with a certain childlike energy!

It was François Mauriac's view that politics did not turn Merton away from God because, he said, "it is because of the things in Heaven that I am involved in the things down here below." But we don't get involved in politics with our heart; we do so with our heads and our nerves. Mauriac was a layperson, who kept himself very well informed and who was counseled (more or less well). Merton was a monk, that is to say, removed from the world. He found himself at grips with a formidable problem: "Give to Caesar what is Caesar's and to God what is God's."

But where is the exact dividing line between what belongs to Caesar and what belongs to God? In some cases it is blurred. What the Pharisees sought to get from Jesus was an answer which would make religion become the ruin of humanity, opposition to the world, an alibi which would allow them to turn away from building the world. In other words, can someone, by wanting to be entirely a man, be truly Christian? Or, again, must he make a choice between being a man or being a Christian?

But to choose in favor of being a man as opposed to being a Christian is, in the end, to choose to be against man. To choose in favor of being a Christian, is, in the end, in spite of appearances, to choose to be in favor of man.

Why? Because man does not define himself only as a "rational animal," but he must add "created in the image and in the likeness of God," that is to say, that man is also the son of God, "part of his divine creation." This participation is sown at the time of our baptism. It is a seed that grows in our souls.

In truth, if there is no human really without a personal relationship with God, by the same reasoning, there is no true civilization—even a technical civilization—without respect and cultivation of a person's values of inner life. Then, if in order to be fully human, one must be Christian, then how can we separate Christian life from social life?

Politics or even the supernatural is nothing more than an optional coat of paint spread onto the human person. God, through the incarnation of his Son, came to save all humanity. To want to cut religion off from its earthly roots is the same as becoming like the Pharisees of yesterday or even today, which would amount to destroying it.

We must, then, put everything into its proper perspective. Everything that is Christian is so because it is totally human. Christ destroyed nothing in the human person—except sin. God fulfills us; he completes us.

God's completion of us means that our life is no longer divided into a portion of humanity, that is, say, profane, and a portion that is Christian. Thus, let us seek to find God in everything: in the problem of hunger, in the poverty of developing countries, in the threats of war, and so on.

This union with God further forces us to put everything in its proper perspective, a point of view that says that God is the first to be served. It is only then that human beings are fulfilled and transformed, that they become completely human because they are completely Christian. In concrete terms, this interactive transformation is not so simple, and achieving this integration raises a thousand and one questions.

Merton's action was generous. He acted in good faith but he was accused of writing from atop an ivory tower; this made him all the more uncertain whether or not his solitude made him more lucid about the problems on which he took a stand or less lucid. Despite these reservations and obstacles, Merton was a profound thinker who had a strong impact on American society and who exerted a great deal of influence.

He was happiest, even more than happy, when he was protesting against the structures of his order. He saw all of the changes that he had advocated, for which he battled with courage, come to be realized, thanks to Vatican II. In this sense, he was a visionary in the monastic realm. This is true, even if he had the impression that some of his insights exceeded his expectations, that they went too far and he, at times, regretted that the changes had not been made in more moderation and serenity.

In the last years of his life, he was even uneasy to see the turn of events and the evolution of reforms. In a book on the forms and nature of monasticism, Merton went into greater detail about these questions, but this is not the time or the place to go into detail about the structures of monastic life.

## REFLECTION QUESTIONS

Can you recall the last issue, event, or circumstance that you felt strongly enough about to express an opinion, even if that opinion was not well received? Do you still feel as strongly about it as you once did? Can you recall an expressed opinion or protest that might now be a cause of regret or embarrassment for you? Have you brought these feelings, and the lessons learned, to your prayer? Can you discover within the experience the stirrings of grace, possibly calling you to something more?

## DAY NINE

# A Meditator

**FOCUS POINT**

"I will meditate on your precepts" (Ps 119). I meditate, because I acknowledge that "God's ways are not my ways" (Isa 55:8), and I meditate so that I may "know the treasures of wisdom and knowledge" (Col 2:3). I reserve the necessary time to reflect, to ponder, to let the word of God, "rich as it is" (Col 3:16), flow over me, through me, and in me, so that I "may have eternal life" (1 Jn 5:13) and live it to the full.

*Some people live for God, some live with God, some in God.*

Thomas Merton, *Thoughts in Solitude*

W e notice a progression in the text cited above. Prayer assures that these passages are safely navigated. In his writings, Merton always sought to teach his readers how to pray, ever mindful of the request from Christ's disciples: "Lord, teach us to pray" (Lk 11:1). This request should often be one made by ourselves with the reminder and knowledge that our friend Tom gives us precious advice.

In his book *Spiritual Direction and Meditation*, Merton first sketches for us a good outline about spiritual direction, its advantages, and its limitations (don't expect too much from this interaction). He then opens to us to the sacred part of meditation by these words: "To meditate is to reflect seriously."

Meditation, Merton believes, is both a mental activity and definite concentration on a specific subject, for example: the Incarnation, Our Lord's Passion, the Cross, death, Mary, the Eucharist, a book, or even a single passage in the Bible, and so on. There are numerous other subjects for meditation: our life, our experiences, our duties, our problems, the presence of Christ and his actions in our life. It is necessary for us to link the ideas about a specific subject together. We must draw support from a passage in the Gospel or from daily Mass. Feelings might spring up, but what is important in this process is faith.

As far as time is concerned, it would be good for us to strive to find some opportunity every day to devote only to the Lord. That is the best way to make progress in matters of the spirit. Merton further says:

Contemplative souls generally have a particular affinity for the presence of God in themselves or for another means to feel the closeness of God in the intimacy of their being.

*Thomas Merton,* Spiritual Direction and Meditation

The guidelines could change: We are able to meditate more easily in the silence of the chapel, of the garden, of a room, or of a forest.

*Thomas Merton,* Spiritual Direction and Meditation

The position of our body should make our meditative effort easier. Merton is quick to tell us in *Spiritual Direction and Meditation* that "naturally, the best position for meditation is the sitting position," and not on our knees.

What is important is to seek silence, tranquility, retreat, peace.

*Thomas Merton,* Spiritual Direction and Meditation

All types of meditation that do not seek to make our being conform to the will of God remain unproductive and abstract. But all types of sincere inner prayer which truly seeks this essential goal—our conformity to the Will of God—could never go without being rewarded by grace and demonstrating one of the most sanctifying forces in our life.

*Thomas Merton,* Spiritual Direction and Meditation

Meditative reflection is only the beginning of an action which leads to inner prayer and should normally result in contemplation.

*Thomas Merton,* Spiritual Direction and Meditation

In two other books, *Seeds of Contemplation* and *New Seeds of Contemplation*, Merton provides an introduction to contemplative prayer. In order to understand the route of contemplation, we can remember the famous adage: reading meditation, prayer contemplation.

It is not necessary to have a method or system for contemplation but to cultivate an attitude or an approach; little by little, the soul will turn itself toward this way: "The path of true prayer" will indicate the way and make us aware of God's loving attention.

Merton taught meditation and prayer because through it, his soul expanded. We are lucky to have such a lucid interpreter.

## REFLECTION QUESTIONS

Do I have a regular practice of meditation? Do I spend time each day meditating on the Word of God and permitting that word to nourish me? What are the necessary steps that might suggest themselves to me in order to begin a regular practice of meditation? Do I record the "fruits" of my meditation in a journal and regularly share them with my spiritual director? Am I open to the will of God revealed to me in this prayer of contemplation?

DAY TEN

# A Spiritual Master

## FOCUS POINT

How can I determine if the person in whom I place my trust can lead me to where I feel that I have been called to go? The difference, illustrated by recalling the example of a routine sports exhibition, is readily determined by asking yourself if your guide is a spectator or a player-coach. A spectator can only report to you what he or she has seen and heard. A player-coach can share with you what to do, accurately access your level of preparation, counsel you about what may come next, prepare you for the inevitable successes and failures, and rejoice with you each step of the way.

*The Mystical Body of Christ is the Body of those who are united with one another and with the Father and the Son by a union of charity so close that it is analogous to the circumincession in which the Father dwells in the Son and the Son in the Father. Indeed, our status as sons of God depends on the fact that our unity with Christ makes the Father dwell in us as He dwells in the Son, while we dwell in the Father as does the Son....The force that holds this unity together is charity.*

Thomas Merton, *The New Man*

I n order to help those who came to him for counsel, to put them in a proper frame of mind for an upcoming retreat, as well as to help them commit to it, inspire them, and bring them to his way of thinking, Merton called upon his own experience: his experience as a monk who was nourished through the Rule of Saint Benedict; the liturgy; and, in particular, *lectio divina*, that is to say, the spiritual reading of the Bible and its great spiritual commentators.

Merton begins with the principle that God alone is enough, a principle that is at the very core of monasticism. What is sought implicitly, if not explicitly, through the desire for God which dwells in the hearts of human beings, is the experience of union with God. Further, Merton taught and wrote nothing other than what he tried to live as a monk. So, as a result, it is understandable that in his books that we read, in detail, about his own spiritual experience.

For a long time, the liturgical year held a place of great importance to Merton. He loved the liturgy, but it wasn't until the last years of his life that he discovered "the one beyond." By patterning himself then on the feast days, he turned his focus to celebrating the mysteries. He sees Christ celebrating the feast in us, and us celebrating in him. Thus occurs a true theophany or a visible manifestation of God to human beings, that is to say, a mysterious manifestation of the Lord through his teachings, through his actions, and through the rites during which the significance of the mystery being celebrated materializes within us.

This celebration is, above all, an action. It does not consist of piously living the events of the liturgical life of Jesus; it consists of celebrating his redemptive work through his total permanent presence. Each of Christ's actions was done for a reason; each is important. To celebrate the mystery is to fulfill it. In this celebration, brought about by the Word which proclaims it, and by the "real symbol" it represents, the celebrator acquires the life-giving contact through the redemptive act of Christ, presented again and reactualized again in order to be united with him and to live through him.

We must start from this point if we want to tackle the problem of the spiritual identity of human persons as revealed in the Bible, the covenant between God and each of us. In *The New Man*, one of the most important books Father Louis wrote on this subject, he explains his views. How can we take possession of our true self? The answer is through a second birth as outlined to Nicodemus on his visit to Jesus in Chapter 3 of John's Gospel. Jesus isn't satisfied just to teach us about a Christian life; he creates it in our souls through the action of the Holy Spirit. Our life in him is then not just a question of good will or perfect morals; it is a completely new spiritual reality, an inner transformation brought about by all of the sacraments and most particularly by baptism and the Eucharist. If we are truly "real only through him," it is because he shares his reality with us and makes it our own.

> When we speak of "life in Christ," according to the phrase of Saint Paul, "It is no longer I who live, but it is Christ who lives in me" (Gal 2:20), we are speaking not of alienation of the self, but of our discovery of our true selves in Christ. In this discovery, we participate spiritually in the mystery of Christ's Resurrection. And this sharing of the death and Resurrection of Christ is the very heart of the Christian faith....
>
> The life He came to bring us is His own life as Son of God. And because of His Resurrection, He received the power to communicate to us all His Spirit as the principle of our own life and the life of our own spirit.
>
> *Thomas Merton,* The New Man

It is up to us, then, to actualize the union with Christ, a union that is vital, dynamic, and spiritual. Christians are no longer beings who live for themselves and who shut themselves in, waiting in their own autonomy, their own absolute sovereignty. Christians are beings who no longer belong only to themselves, but to Christ, living and dying with him, through him, and for him. It is a dynamic union, a fulfilling by an effective power, a vital union created by human persons taking part in God's life, a spiritual union which makes them become one with Him in spirit, which unites them to Him by the tightest bond: the Holy Spirit who, at the same time, enters Christ and the soul of all Christians. Father Louis draws our attention to just how perfect is the symmetry of Christ's relationship with his Father, on the one hand, and how perfect was the symmetry of Christ's relationship with his disciples on the other.

> Christ living in me is at the same time Himself and myself. From the moment that I am united to Him "in one spirit," there is no longer any contradiction implied by the fact that we are different persons.... Christ mystically identifies His members with Himself by giving them His Holy Spirit.
>
> *Thomas Merton,* The New Man

It is through the Eucharist that this union is fulfilled and developed. Merton wrote a lovely book of Thomist inspiration on this subject entitled *The Living Bread*. Here are some of his thoughts from that work.

> By our union with Christ in the Eucharist, we find our true selves. The false self, the "old man," is burned away by the fervor of charity generated by His intimate presence within our soul. And the "new man" comes into full possession of himself as we "live, now not we, but Christ liveth in us."
>
> *Thomas Merton,* The Living Bread

We have seen how Merton points out the traditional doctrine of the Church, based upon Saint John and Saint Paul, in whose writings we see reference to the union between Christ and the Christian. This union is especially fulfilled by the liturgy and more precisely by the Eucharist. But he also knew how to make it come about in a most convincing manner and in a very contemporary style, which was simple, as well as being precise.

## REFLECTION QUESTIONS

What is the difference between being "associated" with and being in "union" with? Is my relationship with the Lord a relationship of union or is it a relationship of association? Do I desire any change in this relationship? In what ways do I feel myself being drawn closer to the Lord? In what ways do I feel myself pulling away from my relationship with the Lord? Do I see my relationship to be both living and dynamic or is there something that is threatening and not life giving that I may be challenged to change? Am I willing to bring the entire relationship to the Lord in prayer? Am I willing to share this relationship with my spiritual director?

# A Precursor of Interreligious Dialogue

## FOCUS POINT

One of the most difficult experiences in the world is to be willing and open enough to share what I deeply hold to be true and necessary with another person who may not agree with me. It is difficult because in order to share honestly with another means that I must be willing to listen. It is in listening that even our deepest held thoughts and convictions can be challenged. Such a challenge is not to be understood as a threat but rather as a respectful and mutual exchange of what each person understands as important and worthwhile.

*Zen intuition is not our consciousness of ourselves by our-*
*selves as if it was of our own doing, but it is the intuition by*
*which the Being finds consciousness of himself in us.*

Thomas Merton, *Mystics and Zen Masters*

*The void of every limited form is the bounty of the One.*

Thomas Merton, *Mystics and Zen Masters*

The missionary epic of the Church throughout the centuries and the sum total of generously accorded sacri-
fices must not be ignored. We must pay homage to all of
those who carried the Good News. However, it is clear that
the evangelistic approach of today is totally different from
that of the past, even the recent past. This approach is less
negative with reference to "the other." What is curious, however, is the fact that the great religions have not as yet faced
this change in approach.

Having seen, however, the extensive mobility of cultures,
we side with the specialists who believe that a great shock
will occur: a confrontation between the religions of Buddhism, Islam, Hinduism, and Christianity. This confrontation will become the major problem of the coming years.

Christianity has, in the course of its two-thousand-year
history, come up against the Roman religion which was never
too strong and the Hellenistic mystery cults which were also
on a declining slope. In an era we will call "colonial" and
even up to today, Christianity collides with animism, fetish-
ism, and agrarian cults tied to various ethnic groups. These
religions have never been too far below the surface.

There was certainly contact between Christianity and Islam in the Middle Ages. Remember that Saint Francis of Assisi met with a sultan and that there were Franciscans martyred by Islamic force. Of course these date are largely episodic.

There was certainly the effort in India in the eighteenth century by the Jesuits of Nobili, who adopted the indigenous customs and found it unseemly to link faith and Christian life solely to Western civilization. This is also episodic. But those who reflect upon the problem of the meaning of other religions within the redemptive plan of Jesus Christ, see the impact as inescapable.

And they say: that's fine.

Vatican II, at the end of paragraph 2 of the document *Nostra Aetate*, "Declaration on the Relation of the Church to Non-Christian Religions," explains it this way:

> The Catholic Church rejects nothing of what is true and holy in these religions. She has a high regard for the manner of life and conduct, the precepts and doctrines which, although differing in many ways from her own teaching, nevertheless often reflect a ray of truth which enlightens all men. Yet she proclaims and is in duty bound to proclaim without fail, Christ who is the way, and the truth, and the life (Jn 14:6). In him, in whom God reconciled all things to himself (2 Cor 5:18–19), men find the fullness of their religious life.

And the Council continues:

> The Church, therefore, urges her sons to enter with prudence and charity into discussion and collaboration with members of other religions. Let Christians,

while witnessing to their own faith and way of life,
acknowledge, preserve, and encourage the spiritual
and moral truths found among non-Christians, also
their social life and culture.

Before Vatican II, the pioneers of such dialogue had
worked along these lines, and we find, among them, Benedictine Father Jules Monchanin (who died in 1957), Dom Henri
le Saux, O.S.B., a Benedictine monk (who died in 1973),
and Thomas Merton (who died in 1968).

Innovations by Monchanin and le Saux, among which was
the establishment of a Christian-Hindu monastic center in South
India, were tentative. But the pace is not as slow today. Other
initiatives have been made that have charted real progress.

In the eyes of some, Merton was truly a forerunner—
certainly very much criticized—and a true artisan of interreligious dialogue.

Whether we like it or not, we live in a time of contact
with different religions of the world. This easy contact ex-
ists, for one reason, because we are less than ten hours from
Calcutta by plane, and for another, because we are better
informed, thanks to a number of seminars, workshops, and
meetings held by these religions.

The stakes are high for Christianity and we must think
about the consequences. Are we ready for this dialogue?
Are we ready to expand the frontiers of the Holy Spirit?
Vatican II pledges us to do just that—as we certainly have
seen—but how do we do it?

We start from a common base of

- dialogue, and
- monasticism.

We begin with dialogue between specialists and, if we rephrase it using Pope Paul VI's words: "the dialogue of salvation," which we can interpret in our way as widespread information.

What are the benefits of this dialogue? They include a discovery of a spiritual thirst, provided that we are prepared for this dialogue and that we do not venture there if we don't know enough about our faith. This venturing into unknown territory could be dangerous, but everything is dangerous: crossing a street courts danger and involves taking a risk.

We must not deny the danger, but perhaps we should plow on. Christians could learn from these people, and deepen, through comparison, our ideas about faith and redemption. We can learn how they view Christ, in comparison to the other paths of freedom, to the irreplaceable role of Christ as the "one mediator between God and humankind" (1 Tim 2:5). Above all, this dialogue makes us understand the other, that is to say, another mentality, another perception of a hunger for the Absolute. Therefore, dialogue should be sought, but we should not harbor any illusions. We are just beginning.

Pope John Paul II also invites us to reflect upon this serious problem when he uses the term "inculturation"—a word which has struck gold in its ability to communicate a new view of the process of dialogue and evangelization. Cardinal Paul Poupard, then archbishop and pro-president of the Secretariat for Non-Believers, said:

> Christ always goes ahead of us in the Galilee of nations…the Gospel is neither occidental nor is it oriental, it is universal. The Church isn't European

or African or Asiatic, it is Catholic...the neologism
[coining of a new word] of inculturation has, for
the first time, been used in an official document,
through a message to God's people at the Bishop's
Synod in the autumn of 1977. This word very well
expresses what is one of the components of the great
mystery of the Incarnation. And it reminds us of
Pope John VI's apostolic admonition (*Evangelii
nuntiandi*) which said: the Gospel and, therefore,
evangelization are most certainly not to be identified with a single culture and are independent with
respect to all cultures. And yet the kingdom, which
is proclaimed by the Gospel, is experienced by men
who are profoundly bound to one culture and the
construction of the kingdom of Heaven may not
borrow elements from culture and human cultures.

What is "inculturation"? Inculturation is the incarnation of the Christian life and message within a tangible cultural area in such a way that not only is this experience
explained using the elements of that particular culture in
question (because that would be only a superficial adapta-
tion), but even more so, that this same experience, itself,
changes into an element of inspiration, which recreates this
culture. In this way, inculturation is the point of origin of a
new creation.

How can we consider this meeting between a message
of universal salvation and a world which is massively identified by a plurality of cultures? Theology could give us one
answer. It should devote itself today to be the theology of
the one Church which is the size of the world.

The possibility of a real inculturation of Christianity in other cultures—in Africa, Latin America, and the Far East—seems to be an extremely difficult question. The Church has not yet sufficiently tackled this issue. Putting orthodoxy aside—but it also belongs to the West in a certain manner—up until the middle of the twentieth century, there was only one European theology "exported" to the entire world. This transmission of European theology to other cultures was a phenomenon which reinforced the wave of "colonialism." However, it is no longer possible to establish the plausibility of Christianity and other cultures on the basis of the superiority of the Western culture. It is, therefore, necessary to build a type of Christianity that presents itself as an essential synthesis with other cultures. This task has already been undertaken, for the Second Vatican Council, composed of an episcopate truly coming from the entire world, did not miss the opportunity of designing the first outlines of a careful theology for universal inculturation.

Christian theology will probably not renew itself through contact with human sciences, but in an approach which is determined by the immense treasures of Hinduism, Judaism, and Islam. A faith in Christ is not just one simple cultural value amid others. There is conflict between the evangelical message and the current culture—a conflict we see as early in Christianity's history as, for example, in Saint Paul's speech before the Areopagus of Athens.

All attempts for total cultural assimilation will always meet with Christian refusal. But we must believe that we can learn something from others because another viewpoint is also a different universe, another spiritual realm. The Upanishads, for example, are a part of the great philosophical-religious texts of India. They were written over numerous centuries in Sanskrit. The most important ones could date back to the five or six centuries before Christ. Little is known of them outside India.

If we are not adaptive to other religions in terms of Christianity, we are also not adequately prepared for the impact that other religions will have on Christianity. We must expand the frontiers of the Holy Spirit, but, nonetheless, we must know how to be careful.

Despite various difficulties we must remember that a well-conducted dialogue could lead to enrichment. And, for goodness sake: we must not extinguish the Holy Spirit in whatever form he takes. We must also carefully recognize "the seeds of the Word" in whatever guise. We must courageously state what draws away from evangelical authenticity and be clear about all that necessitates a conversion.

It is not by osmosis, but by a graft with its vital reactions and the antibodies it creates by which this inculturation should take place. The Church should take on the values of non-Christian cultures in order to understand their religious values, but it also must purify them at the same time. Christ's grace, which transforms human values, also puts them in the proper order so they may be fulfilled. But, above all, what Christianity should bring to non-Christian culture is Jesus himself.

In order to avoid stilted thinking and road-blocked positions, we must prepare for this time; we must enlighten our spirits. Merton predicted this impact, this meeting of different religions; he was a true prophet; and he had the courage to speak up and act on it.

The Christian faith has an opportunity to renew itself through contact with other cultures. This renewal can be compared to a spiritual seeding, exactly like the one in the Word of God in the Gospels, or even better, like the leaven in the dough. For if, in the process of evangelization, Christianity does not make the effort to inculturate, it will be no more than a foreign or outmoded cultural vehicle.

Conversely, if the discussion about faith happens entirely in one particular culture to the point of losing its own identity, that is no longer an evangelical event. Christianity must risk in order to evangelize. Let us then remember the words of Pope John Paul II, said at the beginning of his papacy, words which are often referred to: "Do not be afraid."

So, there is a paradox. There must be a break and a continuity. A break, because the proclamation of the Gospel coincides with the emergence of something new: Christ; and a continuity, because that proclamation is done in the ways, languages, and cultures of those people to whom it is directed.

Merton has placed himself among the precursors and pioneers of the latter part of this century, when the great religious movements question and dialogue with one another. He has indeed opened new roads for the Church. He is one of those stargazers who enlightens a whole life, a great monk, a pioneer of the Christian dialogue with Buddhism, Hinduism, and others. He is a son of Saint Benedict who will always be remembered as a true servant to the will of his spiritual father.

Christianity will undoubtedly emerge triumphant from this encounter with other religions. Has it not survived well after its insertion into the Greek and Latin world of the early centuries? After all, Christianity is attached to no single civilization; not only does it receive something from each, but it makes each productive. Because cultures do not, of themselves, possess the principle of their fulfillment, cultures and religions should experience the mystery of death/resurrection.

Following the publication of Merton's book on Zen, he received a number of letters from notable theologians who urged prudence with regard to encouraging Christians to practice Asian spiritualities.

But Merton felt that for someone who knows his faith well, an exploration of Asian spiritualities could be an enriching experience. Merton wrote this:

> In general, Christians are interested in the positive aspects of God: the creator, the redeemer, providence, justice, love, light. The silences of Zen permit us to also live and fully experience the negative aspect of an absolute and transcendent God. It is not enough to theoretically confess that God transcends our thoughts, we must also live and put our faith in his unthinkable transcendence, by experiencing within ourselves the state of no thoughts and absolute silence, but without abandoning prayer, which addresses itself to the private face of the creator, the redeemer. One day, the grace of illumination will manifest in us the inconceivable unity and supreme logic of the two faces, positive and negative, exterior and interior, of the mystery of God, of a God who reveals himself by remaining hidden and enters into a close relationship while remaining absolutely transcendent. It is by practicing both Zen and prayer at the same time that a Christian will develop his faith in God, who is absolute and the creator.
>
> *Thomas Merton,* Mystics and Zen Masters

*The Cloud of Unknowing* (an anonymous work from the end of the fourteenth century which addresses prayer), about which Merton wrote some nice passages in *Mystics and Zen Masters*, does not seem to be too far removed from what Tom Merton wrote.

## REFLECTION QUESTIONS

As you reflect on your own faith journey, can you recall an experience in which you were faced with a thought or an idea that challenged something that you deeply believed? Can you recall your reaction to such a challenge? Can you recall how you resolved it or does it remain an unresolved question? Have you ever experienced a need to go outside of your own faith tradition? Did you feel nourished, comforted, upset, or troubled by the experience? Did you bring this experience to your prayer?

## DAY TWELVE
# A Pioneer of Intermonastic Dialogue

### FOCUS POINT

What may be possible among strangers is oftentimes not possible among friends and family. The dynamic of family relationships requires a sensitive and cautious approach. "A prophet is not accepted among his own people," the Scriptures teach us. Our own experience of the dynamic of family life underlines the lesson and illustrates the challenge.

---

*Buddha did not say "there is no self."...For he would have said: "Formerly indeed I had a self but now I have not one any more."*

Thomas Merton, *Asian Journal*

*It is no longer I who live, but it is Christ who lives in me.*

Gal 2:20

Intermonastic dialogue is a form of interreligious dialogue and both kinds of dialogue can reinforce each other. Interreligious dialogue can be explored at the level of monasticism. Monasticism is a phenomenon that crosses all of the great religions and which is, in fact and above all, as we have said, a search for interiority, an effort to pull toward the Absolute. Moreover, Hindu and Buddhist monasticisms have existed well before their Christian counterparts, and they are still popular today.

Merton was mainly interested in Buddhism. He met with the Dalai Lama on numerous occasions. The latter wrote: "Thomas Merton was a great master of meditation in the West....When I think of or feel something Christian, an image of him, of his face, appears immediately within me." We can only dream of what a conversation between Merton and Dom le Saux would be like.

In Merton's *Asian Journal*, he outlines all of his contacts. Invited by the organizers of interreligious dialogue and a society whose focus was the implantation of monasticism, Merton was asked to give a presentation at their meeting in Bangkok, Thailand. He died there, on December 10, 1968, on the day that was the anniversary of his entrance into religious life. He died shortly after his presentation, a probable victim of electrocution by a defective fan. It was thought that he had made an attempt to repair the fan, but his total lack of mechanical skills put him in harm's way. He was fifty-three years of age.

In his *Asian Journal*, Merton noted:

> The trip is not concerned with talking, but with learning and with making contact with important people in the Buddhist monastic field. I am essen-

tially interested in Tibetan Buddhism and in Japanese (possibly Chinese) Zen.

*Thomas Merton, Asian Journal*

Merton's approach was to be able to understand another person from his own point of view, from within his own universe of thought. He said: "Those who practice Zen do all that they have to do at leisure. In Gethsemani, it is the same."

A meeting between Christianity and Buddhism is very exacting. Sooner or later, this meeting would have occurred because the Church could not miss the chance to unite hearts with the great Asian spiritual trends. It was also a fortunate thing that certain Christians were called to go ahead toward the actualization of this dialogue.

Assuredly, this intermonastic dialogue was a special vocation, one that cannot be recommended for everyone. It must be done in answer to a clearly recognized calling from God, and solid Christian training must be accomplished in preparation for it. This form of dialogue is always risky, but it is a necessity for the Church of today, and even more so for the Church of the future.

If Christianity can only be understood from the point of view of faith and if we do not allow ourselves to judge non-Christian viewpoints (even for the cause of promoting dialogue), we should still continue. These conditions should not be considered as a strong detraction from the mission, or as expedients to be put into action simply because the proclamation of the Gospel is impossible. Dialogue is an authentic means of giving witness to the Christian faith. A true dialogue between Christians and other believers, however, could only produce a veritable centering of ourselves.

Dialogue is, therefore, not an optional luxury. It is postulated, it seems, by the mysterious action of the Holy Spirit, who is at work in us, but also within our brothers and sisters from different religions.

Didn't Christ himself engage in a dialogue with Nicodemus by night (Jn 3:1 and following)? Did Christ not provide proof, which was patiently discussed; did Christ not listen to his questions and objections because of his availability to everyone? Perhaps the best example of Christ's ability to enter into dialogue is in Chapter 4 of the Gospel of Saint John: the way that Christ proceeded with the woman from Samaria at Jacob's well in Sychar. Christ opens the dialogue, not by bowing to the woman, but by asking for her help, just a little cool water to drink, the least she could offer him. He received before he gave, in this way, beginning the dialogue by an act of humility.

As we have seen, the work of the Gospel is to love our true selves ever more deeply and to help each other in a mutual way to deepen our faith. Christians know that if they have a great deal to give, they will also receive in return. They also know that there is still a great deal to recognize in and understand about Christ, the Word who enlightens every person who comes into this world.

Dialogue is not a polemic nor is it conducted in a proselytic attitude. True dialogue constitutes an innovation in our way of thinking and in our missionary activities. The partisans and opponents of this method meet each other in the process of intermonastic dialogue. The challenge is to maintain the integrity of the group, to work in mutual respect for each other's identity and freedom, as well as to acknowledge each one's missionary attitude and testimony of their faith.

It is only just recently that this kind of dialogue has been discovered to be a formidable theological tool. Doesn't, in fact, our own theology take on a new connotation in light of other religious traditions? Doesn't it bring us to an even greater perception of Christ?

If we are co-pilgrims with the others with whom we dialogue, we must bring to them the fullness of truth, the fullness of the revelation, because human persons define themselves, as we have seen, by the search for the ultimate. Pope John Paul II, following in the footsteps of Paul VI, strongly insisted on this dialogue of truth.

An area of difficulty arises: God, our Savior, "desires everyone to be saved and to come to the knowledge of the truth. For there is one God; there is also one mediator between God and humankind, Christ Jesus..." (1 Tim 2:4–5).

The two affirmations—one that God wants everyone to be saved and one that there is only one mediator between God and humans: Christ—seem to be contradictory because if divine will is truly universal and effective, what means have been foreseen for this salvation? And if religious traditions are the means of salvation, as certain people affirm, what is left of the unique mediation of Jesus Christ? In other words, what is the role of other non-Christian religions (Hinduism, Buddhism, and Islam with many millions of followers each) in the redemptive plan of Jesus Christ? And why do these other religions exist?

The singularity of Christianity is not diminished by saying that other religions have value—that would be an error—or that the other religions are, in themselves, paths for redemption—another error—nor do we have to choose what pleases us in these religions and discard the remainder in favor of finding a common denominator or a fusion of different doctrines as in a sort of New Age syncretism, but we must simply enter into a dialogue with other religions, since being in that dialogue is an aspect of our mission today. Merton made us aware of all of these kinds of problems.

In view of the extreme mobility of people in today's world, one may find oneself seated next to a Muslim or a Buddhist at school or at work. This juxtaposition is even more pronounced in newer cities and suburbs. And if we are taking Catechism courses, certain questions about these other religions may arise. All three—Hinduism, Islam, and Buddhism—aim for the Absolute, but do not believe in the same God. For the Asian religions, ultimate reality is not personal; for Islam, the incarnation is unthinkable since Christ is, at best, a prophet in their eyes.

It is our task to reconcile our Christian faith, which is absolute, with a certain overture to other religions, without changing the perspective of our commitment. The various monasticisms could lead the way for this dialogue.

In sum, Merton was courageously committed to the goal of intermonastic dialogue, and he carefully studied the works of Saint John of the Cross, taking him as sort of a mentor since he was an advocate for the meeting of religions.


## REFLECTION QUESTIONS

Do I enjoy discovering something new? Do I have a spirit of adventure and the desire to learn new things? Do I have the inner conviction and necessary courage to take a risk? Do I prefer safety and routine above all other things? Recall a time when you chose to risk and reflect on your thoughts and feelings as a result of this choice. Recall a time when you chose not to risk and reflect on your thoughts and feelings as a result of this choice.

## DAY THIRTEEN
# A Mystic

FOCUS POINT

Mysticism is often defined as "the science of love" or some-times simply as "being in love with God." Some people feel that mysticism is an experience of life that is reserved for a chosen few. Others believe that mysticism is a necessary experience for all people and that without mysticism the fullness of the human experience can never be reached.

*To understand the sanctity and doctrine of Saint John of the Cross, the first thing we must do is to see them in the clear perspective of the New Testament, the Sermon on the Mount, the profound discourses in the Gospel of Saint John, and particularly the mystery of the Passion and the Resurrection of the Son of God.*

Thomas Merton, *Disputed Questions*

*All the doctrine of Saint John of the Cross is aimed at this ideal balance of the human and the divine: a balance that is to be attained, however, not on a humanistic level, but "in the Spirit."*

Thomas Merton, *Disputed Questions*

———

T homas Merton read a great deal of the writings of Saint John of the Cross. In him, he found a beacon to show the way to the Absolute. The doctrine of Saint John of the Cross is contained within the teachings of Christ:

> If any want to become my followers, let them deny themselves and take up their cross and follow me. For those who want to save their life will lose it, and those who lose their life for my sake, and for the sake of the Gospel, will save it.
>
> *Mark 8:34–35*

All of the writings of John of the Cross teach us to follow Jesus to the very end. Aware of this fact, Thomas Merton in his book *Ascent to Truth* perceives the necessity of having the ordinary desire "to imitate Christ in all things, so that by conforming ourselves to his life we must deny our own, in order to know how to imitate him and behave like Christ would have done in all things."

We must, then, conclude the second task: take up the cross. For as Merton also says in *Ascent to Truth*: "Whatever the taste this may offer to our senses, if it is not done purely for the honor and glory of God, we must renounce and deprive ourselves of that for the love of Jesus Christ."

In other words, he means to say that deprivation is not effective, but affective. He cautions us to use everything as if we were using nothing, forming no attachment to things, because the desire to possess torments us and defiles the soul, weakening the strength of our desire for God.

From Merton we must know that attachments develop, tastes for certain things arise knowingly, voluntarily, and out of habit, precisely at the point when God asks us for the sacrifice of them. We must not be attached to, or set our hearts on, or become enamored with, or would like to possess, or stake our happiness on any of these fleeting things. They all should be swallowed by the abyss which is our faith. However, the soul does not condemn anything that has been created; it renounces that thing, so as not to weigh God against a created good—that would be to wrong him.

Why such a renouncement? Because, without a doubt, all creatures have a certain relationship with God; and they remember, more or less, some remnants of his being according to the degree of perfection in their nature. But between God and them there is no relationship, no essential resemblance. That is why reason cannot unite itself to God by human means, because there is not enough similarity.

The path to God is one single path of pure faith. It is the path which makes us relive the entire paschal mystery of Christ's death and Resurrection, which is the very essence of Christianity.

Let us fulfill the conditions. God cannot go back on his word. What is important is not to torture the Lord of the dance, not to give up prayer, not to give up meditation (for those who are called to do so), but to passively keep oneself in a loving wait for God, not fearing what God may ask of us, and still knowing how to throw ourselves into the water. There is only one way to do this: beg. Learn to receive manna. These are the brush strokes that make the painting complete.

Contemplation which is born out of faith, accompanied by charity, forms a union with God. Then, little by little, because of the darkness (active and passive), the soul is established in divine life, on the condition that the baring of the spirit is practiced to the detriment of the ideas which do not steer it toward God.

In prayer, this same baring process should be practiced all the way to the sacrifice of distinct thoughts so that a general knowledge of God and of everything in him will rise in the soul.

In effect, the soul that is free from attachments in spirit, heart, and feelings offers God a field, free and disengaged of all shackles, in which he can divinely operate. The soul has nothing more to do than to passively receive this operation from God, which happens in its very depths. It should not be stopped by the distaste which could invade it at certain times, but it should continue on the path by always supporting itself more by faith.

Saint John of the Cross used the comparison of the window in order to signify that there, where there is no distinct knowledge or preconceptions or blockages, the light of God can pass through. In his book *Ascent to Truth*, Merton describes very well the complete itinerary of the ascension of the Carmelite spirituality.

However, the Gospel is a word, sown into the ground, so that a free, personal resurgence can occur. In the same way, to a certain extent, there is a possibility left open for each person to write their own story through the writings of Saint John of the Cross.

There is the written Gospel—the books—and the sung Gospel—life.

Saint John of the Cross was a man of the sixteenth century; he is also contemporary. We must make an effort to remove ourselves from our current culture in order to reach the core of his work. We must concern ourselves, with the help of his writings, to become free, not to bring Saint John of the Cross up to date, but to live our lives of today with the Spanish Doctor.

There are as many different vocations as there are people, as we have seen, but each person, if they want to go toward the absolute of God, above all, if they want to reach the Absolute, they must approach it by the way of purification—a darkness of feeling and spirit, active and passive—which could also take on some very new and diverse forms.

Each one of us—in our own way—must write his or her own story. A good place to start is by reading about Saint John of the Cross. That is what Merton invites us to do in his book, which he dedicated to the author of the book called *The Living Flame of Love.*

## REFLECTION QUESTIONS

What are you attached to? If you were to make a listing of all those things, people, events, and experiences that you hold as important, which of them would you list from one through five? Now, can you take each of these "attachments" to the Lord in prayer and slowly let them go? Reflect on the process that you went through in composing your list and record the feelings you experienced. You are now prepared to begin the process of writing your story.

## DAY FOURTEEN
# An Apostle
# of Contemplation

### FOCUS POINT

Live in the present moment, the now, in love. Contemplation is the present moment. It is the experience of not worrying about what has been or thinking about what might happen next. Contemplation is the experience of being totally present to what you are doing at this very moment. If you present to the now, and you are present in love, you are present to God.

*Within this deep self, my personal solitude meets that of men and that of God.*

Thomas Merton, *Disputed Questions*

Thomas Merton read a great deal and retained a great deal. He particularly liked the Cistercian authors. The better known ones include Saint Bernard (about whom we have already written); William of Saint Thierry (1085–1148); Aelred of Rievaulx (1109–1167); Isaac de l'Étoile (an abbot in 1147, he lived a little longer after the death of Saint Bernard); and Guerric d'Igny (who died in 1157).

It seems that Merton particularly liked *The Golden Letter* or *The Letter to the Brothers at Mont-Dieu* by William of Saint Thierry. Saint Thierry, a Benedictine at Saint Nicaise de Reims, wanted to embrace the reform of Cîteaux, much in the same manner as Merton. He aspired to more solitude, like Merton, and Merton found himself secure with him.

Saint Thierry's point that "to believe in Christ is to go to Him by loving Him" could sum up all of Merton's actions. Merton also became passionately fond of the famous formula: *amor ipse notitia est-amor ipse intellectus* (love itself is knowledge). He continued, like his painter-artist father, by successive strokes of the brush, to paint his ideas in a creative progression. His thoughts form no system. In no way did he want to be an architect. Merton was fascinated by God, and he had an immense and untiring curiosity concerning the approaches which would take him to God. He sought and he found (Mt 7:7), but he wanted to find even more, from a new search. All of this was thanks to *lectio divina*, reading each word slowly, savoring it, as if God spoke to us through the pages, and also to his life of prayer.

He greatly liked the maxims of the Desert Fathers, the first monks who were full of sensible ideas and spirituality, and who gave their visitors certain "words for life," or wisdom of the desert.

In his book *Disputed Questions*, Merton invites us to read the works of Saint John of the Cross, Cistercian works, *The Cloud of Unknowing*, and the spiritual writings from Mount Athos and the Sinai. In *The Sign of Jonas*, he wrote:

> Yesterday, in the confessional, Dom Gildas said a lot of good things and it would be well not to forget them. So I write them down:
>
> I ought to try to understand contemplation, and especially to let people know, in what I write, that the contemplative life is quite easy and accessible and does not require extraordinary or strange efforts, just the normal generosity required to strive for sanctity.
>
> *Thomas Merton,* The Sign of Jonas

Merton followed this advice and magnificently accomplished it, citing the Gospel of John, chapter 14:21, 23: "Those who love me will be loved by my Father, and I will love them and reveal myself to them....My Father will love them, we will come to them and make our home with them." Merton also wrote:

> Perhaps not everyone in the monastery will arrive at a real recognition of this intimate presence of God: but I hardly think it possible that God would allow men to devote themselves entirely to seeking Him without letting them, in some way or other, find Him. I think He wants many of us to find Him and realize Who it is that we have found.
>
> *Thomas Merton,* The Sign of Jonas

These words should help all readers—no matter who they are—in their search for God.

In the last chapters of *Seeds of Contemplation*, Merton clearly showed how the soul in infused contemplation (that which is given by God) was, at times, functioning at its highest level of activity (love) and less and less conscious of this activity to the point of no longer experiencing the loving action of God on it.

For Merton, contemplation is, in itself, an apostolate. He truly believed that a soul united to God could participate in his work of the sanctification and redemption of the world for as John says (15:5): "Those who abide in me and I in them bear much fruit." Merton knew how to invite and to encourage us to seek, no matter what the price.

## REFLECTION QUESTIONS

Have I ever fully experienced the present moment, the now? In the experience of the now did I discover and acknowledge the fullness of the presence of God? Do I find my heart and my soul longing to return to this moment? Am I willing to take the necessary steps and engage in the everyday practice that will lead me once again to contemplation? Am I willing to let go of the thoughts, actions, and attachments that lead me further and further away from the present moment?

## DAY FIFTEEN
# A Traveling Companion

## FOCUS POINT

Any journey, no matter the distance, can oftentimes be experienced best with a traveling companion. A companion is helpful with all of the necessary and mundane tasks that are an essential part of the experience of travel. A companion is also a person with whom we can share our thoughts and impressions, but most of all, they can be a wonderful resource for remembering. When we are able to share our journey with another, we are somehow also enriched and nourished.

*And I believe that by openness to Buddhism, to Hinduism, and to these great Asian traditions, we stand a wonderful chance of learning more about the potentiality of our own traditions.*

Thomas Merton, *Asian Journal*

Thomas Merton actualized Pope Paul VI's wish, which he declared while addressing himself to the sons of Saint Benedict, "Make others aware of, so that they can benefit from, the results of your religious experience, by publishing beautiful books about true Catholic spirituality" (October 16, 1966). The books authored by the monk from Gethsemani were a reminder, for the world of today, to look to the heavens.

Merton equally actualized the hopes of Vatican II as expressed in the *Nostra Aetate* declaration, previously cited.

Thomas Merton opened the frontiers of the spirit. Here is an extract of an informal talk that Merton gave in Calcutta in October 1968:

Behind, then, all that I have said is the idea that significant contacts are certainly possible and easy on the level of experience, not necessarily institutional monasticism, but among people who are seeking. The basic condition for this is that each be faithful to his own search.

And so I stand among you as one who offers a small message of hope, that first, there are always people who dare to seek on the margin of society, who are not dependent on social acceptance, not dependent on social routine, and prefer a kind of free-floating existence under a state of risk. And among these people, if they are faithful to their own calling, to their own vocation, and to their own message from God, communication on the deepest level is possible.

And the deepest level of communication is not communication, but communion. It is wordless. It is beyond words, and it is beyond speech, and it is beyond concept. Not that we discover a new unity. We discover an older unity. My dear brothers, we are already one. But we imagine that we are not. And what we have to recover is our original unity. What we have to be is what we are.[2]

*Thomas Merton*, Asian Journal

To summarize our fifteen-day retreat with Thomas Merton, we could read this following prayer which summarizes the man and his work:

This prayer was offered at the First Spiritual Summit Conference in Calcutta by Thomas Merton:

### CLOSING PRAYER

I will ask you to stand and all join hands in a little while. But first, we realize that we are going to have to create a new language of prayer. And this new language of prayer has to come out of something which transcends all our traditions, and comes out of the immediacy of love. We have to part now, aware of the love that unites us, the love that unites us in spite of real difference, real emotional friction....The things that are on the surface are nothing, what is deep is Real. We are creatures of love. Let us therefore join hands, as we did before, and I will try to say something that comes out of the depths of our hearts. I ask you to concentrate on the love that is in you, that is in us all. I have no idea what I am going to say. I am going to be silent a minute, and then I will say something....

Oh God, we are one with You. You have made us one with You. You have taught us that if we are open to one another, You dwell in us. Help us preserve this openness and to fight for it with all our hearts. Help us to realize that there can be no understanding where there is mutual rejection. Oh God, in accepting one another wholeheartedly, fully, completely, we accept You, and we thank You, and we adore You, and we love You with our whole being, because our being is in Your being, our spirit is rooted in Your spirit. Fill us then with love, and let us be bound together with love as we go our diverse ways, united in this one spirit which makes You present in the world, and which makes You witness to the ultimate reality that is love. Love has overcome. Love is victorious. Amen.

*Thomas Merton,* Asian Journal

We find ourselves living in a time of troubling contradictions and instability; on the one hand, we live in a society where the motto "use it and throw it away" reigns, where we use as many planetary resources as possible, and on the other hand, we live in a society where an ever-growing number of people are acutely aware of the vicious circle that is created by this same mentality. This second group finds themselves seeking—not always explicitly—what is truly essential in our "divine core" and the meaning of our existence.

Saint Benedict has something to say about this, which is perhaps much more important to the world of today. He taught, through his Rule, how we can get to the center of our "heart," how we can "dwell within ourselves," and, as well, he proposes some reflections about the direction of our lives.

Thomas Merton, this Trappist from the heartland of America, has delivered his message which we have followed during this retreat in a meditative synthesis.

In the type of consumer-oriented society in which we are currently living, we must know how to get drawn to the "deeper self." He outlined, in simple terms, the paths we can follow to the One who is the only essential to our lives, in terms which are relevant to our times, and addressed these words to a general population. He is oriented toward the center of the soul, he knew how to awaken modern man to his dimension of interiority, which is the foundation of the human person, and as well, he knew how to develop "the spirit of the soul" that sleeps in each of us. Like Jacques Maritain, he revealed, in his own way and in our times, the importance of a contemplative spirit.

It is the mission of the great religious personalities to reflect back the conflicts and world suffering they see in our current society. They "feel" this world, by living at their own pace, at times leaving it all behind, to carry the cross. This is true for Thomas Merton, as it was once true for Bernard of Clairvaux and so many others. And when they speak of the love of God, it is because they have felt it like a living reality.

In conclusion, here are a few testimonials. Above all is one from Dom Jacques Winandy, former Benedictine abbot, who founded a colony of hermits in Canada.

> It is thanks to him [Merton] that the Trappists have taken the aspirations of eremitical life, which manifests itself among their monks, seriously. He greatly

desired, at a certain time, to go to a more solitary order. But that was not his path because it is undeniable that his vocation was one of being a spiritual writer and prophet, in the sense that he knew how to look at and analyze the problems of his time in the light of God....He followed the path, which was outlined for him, by his monastic vocation, and the exceptional gifts which were given to him. But this path, wasn't it really outlined by God?

*Dom Jacques Winandy,*
*Letter written to the author, April 25, 1996*

For Marie Madeleine Davy, Thomas Merton was "a profound spirit who had an immense influence on American Catholicism. He had a certain charisma, but at times perhaps lacked a certain amount of judgment. He was not always well 'seen' where he was because of his political ideals."

For Dom Pierre Miguel, the former abbot of Ligugé, Thomas Merton appeared to be "a good popularizer for the monastic tradition in the current world of today."

## REFLECTION QUESTIONS

Use these questions to evaluate your fifteen days with Thomas Merton: What happened to me during these days? What struck me as important? What did I feel about what I read? What was my mood? Did I notice any changes in my mood? What did the Lord show me? Was any particular spiritual path revealed to me? Are there any particular points that I might need to return to for more reflection and prayer? What do I most want to remember? Do I feel the need to make any resolution or commitment as the result of these days of prayer?

# Bibliography

THOMAS MERTON wrote many books—there are currently at least sixty in print in English (many of which have been translated into numerous languages). What we will try to do, in this present bibliography, is to note especially his books which have been cited in each chapter.

*The Ascent to Truth*. New York: Harcourt Brace, 1951.

*The Asian Journal of Thomas Merton*. New York: New Directions, 1973.

*Bread in the Wilderness*. Philadelphia: Fortress Press, 1986.

*Collected Poems of Thomas Merton*. New York: New Directions, 1987.

*Conjectures of a Guilty Bystander*. New York: Doubleday, 1966.

*Contemplation in a World of Action*. New York: Doubleday, 1971.

*Contemplative Prayer*. New York: Doubleday (Image Books), 1992.

*Disputed Questions*. San Diego: Harcourt Brace Jovanovich, 1985.

*Exile Ends in Glory: The Life of a Trappistine, Mother M. Berchmans, O.C.S.O.* Milwaukee: Bruce Publishing, 1948.

*Faith and Violence: Christian Teaching and Christian Practices*. Notre Dame, Ind.: University of Notre Dame Press, 1968.

*The Last of the Fathers: Saint Bernard of Clairvaux and the Encyclical Letter, Doctor Mellifluus*. New York: Harcourt Brace Jovanovich, 1981.

*Life and Holiness*. New York: Herder & Herder, 1963.

*Living Bread*. New York: Farrar, Straus & Cudahy, 1956.

*Monastic Peace*. Abbey of the Gethsemani: 1958.

*Mystics and Zen Masters*. New York: Farrar, Straus & Giroux, 1967.

*The New Man*. Noonday Press, 1978.

*No Man Is an Island*. New York: Harcourt Brace Jovanovich, 1955.

*Praying the Psalms*. Collegeville, Minn.: Liturgical Press, 1956.

*The Road to Joy: The Letters of Thomas Merton to New and Old Friends*. New York: Harcourt Brace, 1993.

*The Secular Journal of Thomas Merton*. New York: Farrar, Straus & Cudahy, 1959.

*Seeds of Contemplation*. New York: New Directions, 1986.

*Seeds of Destruction*. New York: Farrar, Straus & Giroux, 1964.

*The Seven Storey Mountain*. San Diego: Harcourt Brace Jovanovich, 1990.

*The Sign of Jonas*. New York: Octagon Books, 1983.

*Silence in Heaven: A Books of the Monastic Life*. London: Thames & Hudson, 1956.

*The Silent Life*. New York: Farrar, Straus & Cudahy, 1957.

*Spiritual Direction and Meditation*. Collegeville, Minn.: Liturgical Press. 1960.

*Thoughts in Solitude*. Boston: Shambhala, 1993.

*The Waters of Siloe.* New York: Harcourt Brace Jovanovich, 1979.

*Silence in Heaven: A Book of Monastic Life.* New York: Crowell, 1956.

*What Are These Wounds? The Life of a Cistercian Mystic: Saint Lutgarde of Aywieres.* Milwaukee: Bruce Publishing, 1950.

# Notes

1. Clervaux is in the Grand Duchy of Luxemburg, not to be confused with Clairvaux which is in the Burgundy region of France (where, in 1115, the monks of Cîteaux founded an abbey).

2. This prayer is of the type common in Rheno-Flemish spirituality which flourished in Belgium and the Rhineland in the thirteenth century. The Rhineland mystics sought God in the center of their being.